DANCER GLORY

ART BY CARA LESLIE BERTON

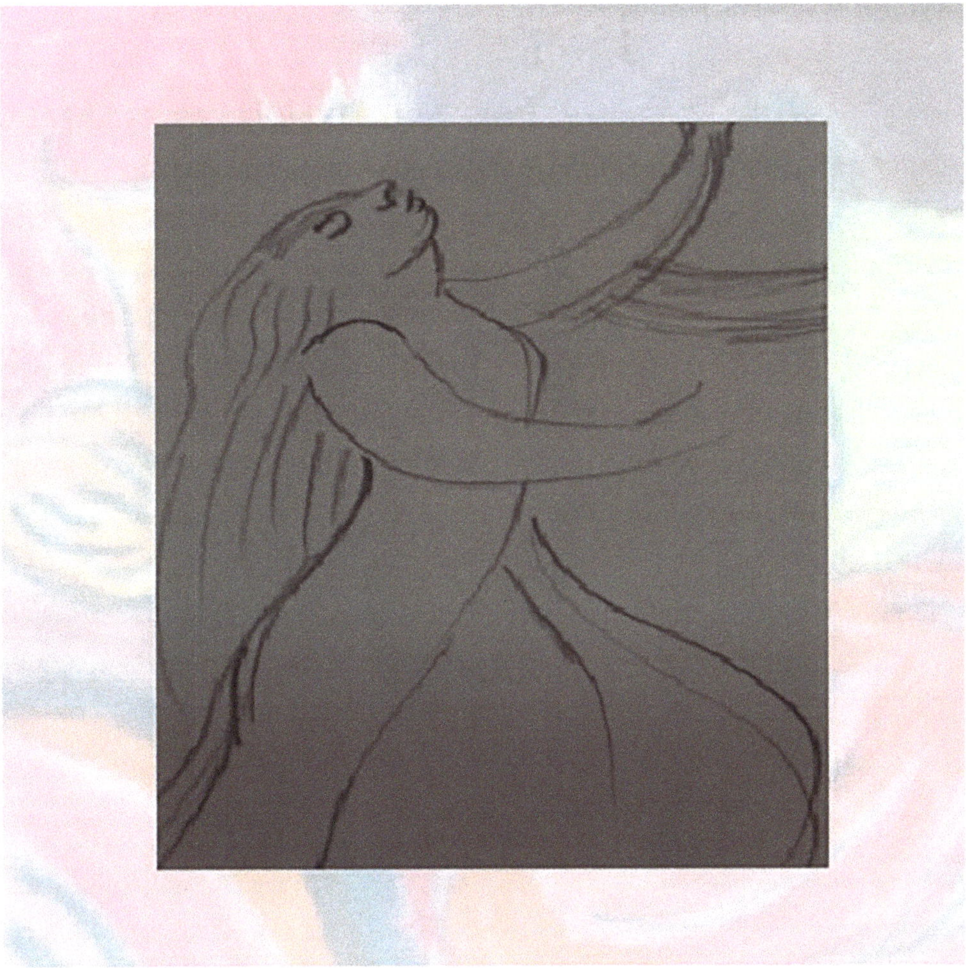

Rose Press
Oakland, California

RESPONSES TO *DANCER GLORY*

Cara Berton ... Her Heart and Art

"Cara has shared her multi-media creations since the mid 1970s. Her craft is her ability to reveal her deepest thoughts...her powerful reactions to experiences. Her subjects span the spectrum of still life, nature, the sky and the other-worldly. However, her greatest focus has been on the details of the people.

Cara uses black and white to represent despair and her struggle against the evils and obstacles of everyday life; and she uses dramatic colors to express her enthrallment with the joy of persons, real and represented in religious contexts. And interspersed with all the images is the occasional expression of Cara's inner life through poetic verses which reveal her superb command of the English language.

"Her prolific interpretation of the world of real people and that of her imagination shines through the laser-like images she sends me regularly via email! What a joy it's been to be on the receiving end of Cara's creativity!

To truly understand Cara's art, take a moment to read her own words on the subject!" [See "Preface by the Artist"]

—Jerry Zacks, MD

A Blessing for Us Now and for Generations to Come

"Cara is so talented, and truly loves to express herself in poetry and art, as these are precious gifts The Lord has truly given her to share with us. I pray that you, too, are truly blessed by her work and Masterpieces, because she has truly become one of The Masters' Masterpieces.

Art by Cara is a blessing for us now and for generations to come as we share with our loved ones the gift God blessed her with, so share Cara's work with your loved ones to double the blessing. I pray you too are as blessed as I am in viewing this marvelous work of art."

—Linda Floyd, Advanced Certified Christian Counselor and Life Coach

FOREWORD

If you want to give your heart a good exercising, the art of Cara Berton will help you with that. In our highly accomplishment-focused culture, the surface of life may be all we get to be presented with, while our hearts have to live under the radar. So we don't get to know our hearts in their deeper, more longing capacities, and where that longing might lead us—into the darkness, but also through the darkness into light; into our human loneliness, but also through our loneliness into love and a larger Belonging.

Cara's art opens us into that fertile territory of the heart. Her subjects include love and intimacy, suffering and redemption, family, longing and belonging (both human and religious), nostalgia, nature, the angelic world, aging, beauty, and more. And because she communicates all this through the wordless medium of her artwork, we get to encounter certain feeling places in our own hearts that we might not otherwise recognize. When we are conditioned to the glossy surface of ourselves, how much of us beneath the surface goes hungry? *Someone* has to paint the subtler realities of feeling, in its many dimensions—as Van Gogh did, as Rembrandt did—for us to know the fullness of ourselves and who we might become.

Cara Berton's drawings and paintings give us this. The lines drawn by her pen and her brush are able to evoke both a primal loneliness and a holy longing for belonging and wholeness. This longing takes both a human form and a religious form, and the many evocative drawings of Jesus in this collection should speak not only to devout Christians but also to people with other faiths, or even no religious faith. If you look at the postures and expressions of the Jesus pictures, you will find in many of them such a profound sense of tenderness and compassion that they invite you to trust in the reality of goodness and forgiveness and transcendence.

The exquisite gentleness of Jesus' expression in drawing #9, "Jesus and Beggar Woman"—doesn't that just capture the encompassing kindness we all long for, from that place in us that feels not quite good enough? And in #35, "Jesus Coming Back," there is a light and a knowing in Jesus' eyes that do seem to promise a world lifted up from the sorrows on earth.

Sometimes the Jesus in Cara's art is stark, in the deeply suffering part of the journey, as in #4, "If This Cup," or #38, "The Cross," and #5, "Darkened Prophet." But more often, Jesus is the Comforter, the Light, the Gatherer into Belonging (as in #39, "Jesus and the Children"), the Resurrector (as in the light-hearted #65, "Jesus Stars"), and other divine aspects whose reality we seek to know more directly.

Other religious figures also appear, movingly. In #63, "Mary and Angels and Me," everything fits together in a curve of the heart's arms, including the Dove of Peace. In #29, "Angels Calling," there *does* look to be a call from these light-filled beings, who are not bound by human gravity. And in #18, "Angel in

My Darling," the angelic aspect that can shine out from a human appears not only in the halo but also in the person's kind and self-reflective expression.

Viewing these images is a personal experience, and I don't want to limit you to seeing the art in categories. But to the extent that these may be useful for you, here are some categories, or contexts, that you might consider when you view the images:

– **Love and Intimacy:**

#14, "The Cuddle Bugs"; #21, "Come Closer to Me"; #22, "The Warmth of Sharing Space"; #27, "Adam and Eve"; #30, "Dramatic Man and Woman"; #31, "Joseph, You Are My Beloved"; #47, "I and Thou"; #51, "My Solitary Love"; #59, "She Is Within Him"; #69, "Two in Love"; #75, "In Love"; #94, "Mother and Child, Jubilant"; and #96, "Loving."

– **Family:**

#10, "My Jewel of My Young Mother"; #11, "Family in a Whirlwind"; #43, "Mordechai Baer"; #44, "Warm Face of My Mother"; #45, "In This World of Touch and Go"; #60, "Portrait of My Father"; #95, "The Last Time I Saw My Mother"; and #98, "My Loving Parents When They Were Young"

– **On a Journey:**

#3, "Growing Old"; #6, "Born Within a Young Girl"; #12, "Labyrinth Dream"; #24, "Alone, Solitary"; #25, "Seeking God"; #46, "Walking Towards Hope"; #59, "She Is Within Him"; #66, "A Strong Woman"; #67, "Moorman"; #71,

"Aging Along"; #72, "Forlorn"; #79, "Deep Thoughts"; #82, "Woman Writing";
#84, "The Quiet Sufferers"; #90, "Child of the Sun"; and #93, "Light Body."'

– **Portraits:**

#3, "Growing Old"; #7, "Portrait of a Fragment of a Man"; #13, "Self-Portrait"; #17, "Self-Portrait"; #32, "Self-Portrait"; #36, "Portrait of David"; #42,
"Pensive"; #50, "Joe"; #51, "My Solitary Love"; #58, "Portrait of Joseph";
#60, "Portrait of My Father"; #89, "Drawing of Joe"; and #97, "Gandhi-Like"

– **Flowering:**

#33, "Birth of a Flower"; #34, "Pregnant Flower"; #52, "Red Flower of Love";
#55, "Flower in Atmosphere"; #80, "Young Flower"; #86, "Summer Bloom";
and #87, "Classic Rose"

– **Nature from an Urban Window:**

#53, "Sun and the Feminine Glory"; #54, "Sky and Covering Tree"; and #88,
"Dawn Over Harlem"

– **Beauty, Joy, and Whimsy**

#15, "Befriending Women"; #19, "Lyrical Dancers"; #20, "The King and His
Children"; #26, "Sparrows of My Heart"; #28, "Dancer Glory"; #57, "People,
Hearts, Stars"; #69, "Two in Love"; #73, "Beautiful"; #83, "Beloved Color";
#85, "Loving Lady and Dignitary"; and #94, "Mother and Child, Jubilant"

– **Cover Art:**

The painting on the cover of this book is #75, "In Love." Another version on the same theme is #61, "Love Is an Emblem."

These categories don't include every image in this book, nor are they meant to be the only way to cohere the images. I offer them mainly to give a sense of both the sweep of Cara's subjects, and to gather them in a way they may be seen to go together, like a bouquet of flowers in a vase. (And there *is* a vase painting: #62, "Victorian Vase.")

I have had many years to become familiar with this artist's work, track its journey, appreciate its beauty and power, and allow it to evolve my heart. The artist is my sister, so I've known her from the start. I have some sense of the hurdles she's been faced with, and what she has had to excavate from within herself, as well as extricate herself from, in order to become the person she is now and to be able to bring forth the depth and the beauty, the perseverance and the faith, that these images reflect. As you go through this book, may you find in these graphic expressions what your own heart, soul, and spirit need for your own healing journey.

—Naomi Rose
Oakland, California

PREFACE BY THE ARTIST

My art has become a means to express spirit.

A portrait of Jesus, a young girl, an aging man ... with an emphasis on the insides of them all.

My vision of Jesus may be very distant in resemblance to his real appearance. My heart belongs to who he truly was, compassion way beyond what we think is possible, omnipotence beyond understanding. These are some of the qualities I try to portray as I create the lines that compose my images of the Lord.

My rather dark pictures come from terror that rises in me, reliving trauma and nightmarish memories. From a dream to a visual image, the unspoken spirit leads the artist in me to link fear with forgiveness.

Once again, I remind myself that the image of Jesus marks the word: "Love thy neighbor as thyself." "Judge not, lest ye be judged."

So we travel on ... adding lines and colors as markers of God creating the universe. From nothing to creation ... through my pen flows the imagery of humankind throughout various moods, relationships, and positions.

Oh take hold, artist ... find the act of creating an inheritance from God.

—Cara Leslie Berton

ILLUSTRATIONS

82. Woman Writing
83. Beloved Color
84. The Quiet Sufferers
85. Loving Lady and Dignitary
86. Summer Bloom
87. Classic Rose
88. Dawn Over Harlem
89. Drawing of Joe
90. Child of the Sun
91. Jesus in Full Color
92. Joyous Flower
93. Light Body
94. Mother and Child, Jubilant
95. The Last Time I Saw My Mother
96. Loving
97. Gandhi-Like
98. My Loving Parents When They
      Were Young

To order copies of this book /
to order prints

THE ART

1. Emotive Jesus

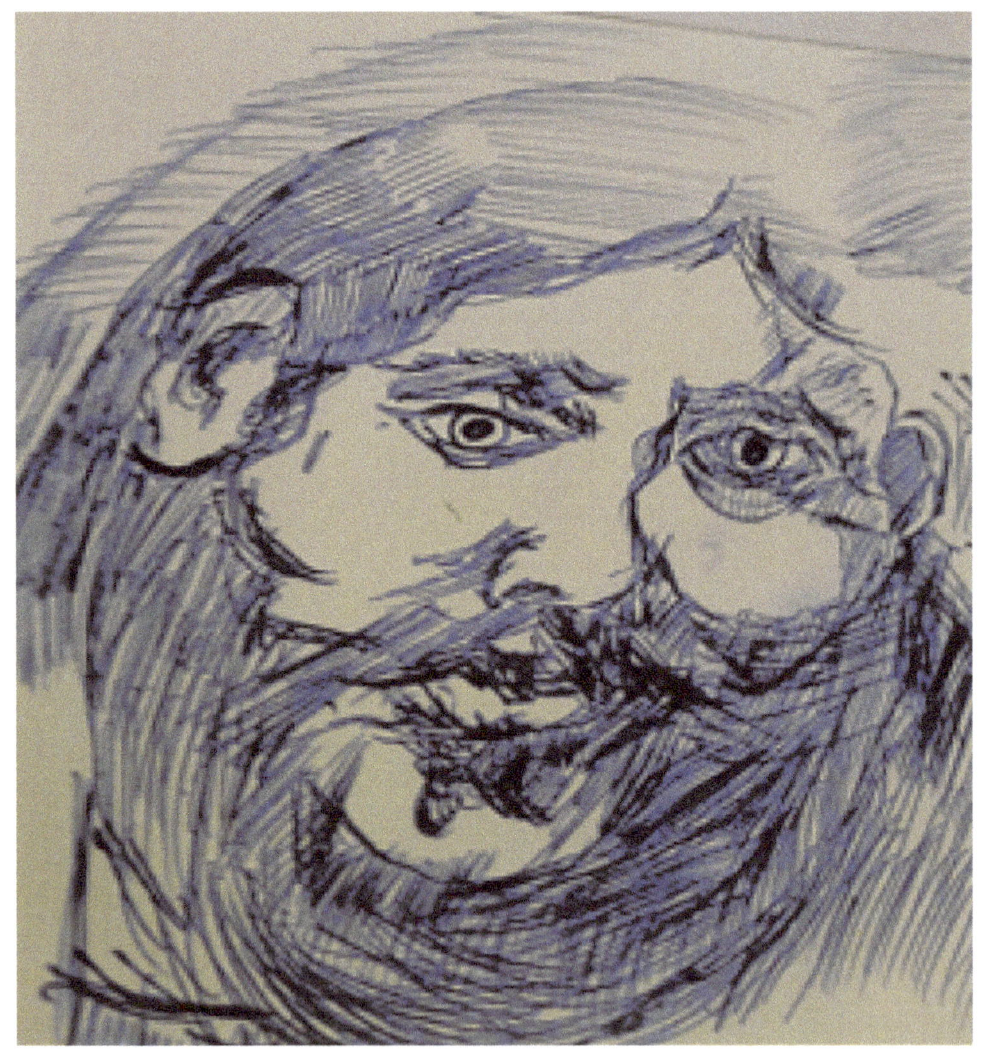

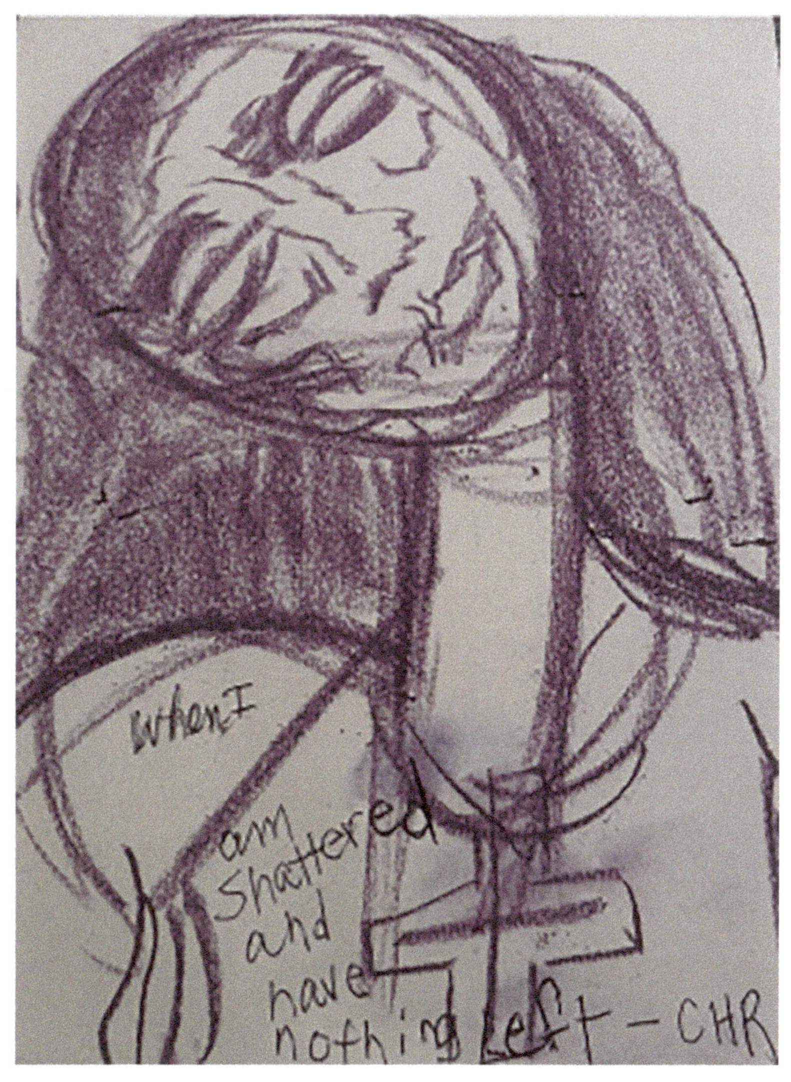

when I
am
shattered
and
have
nothing left — CHR

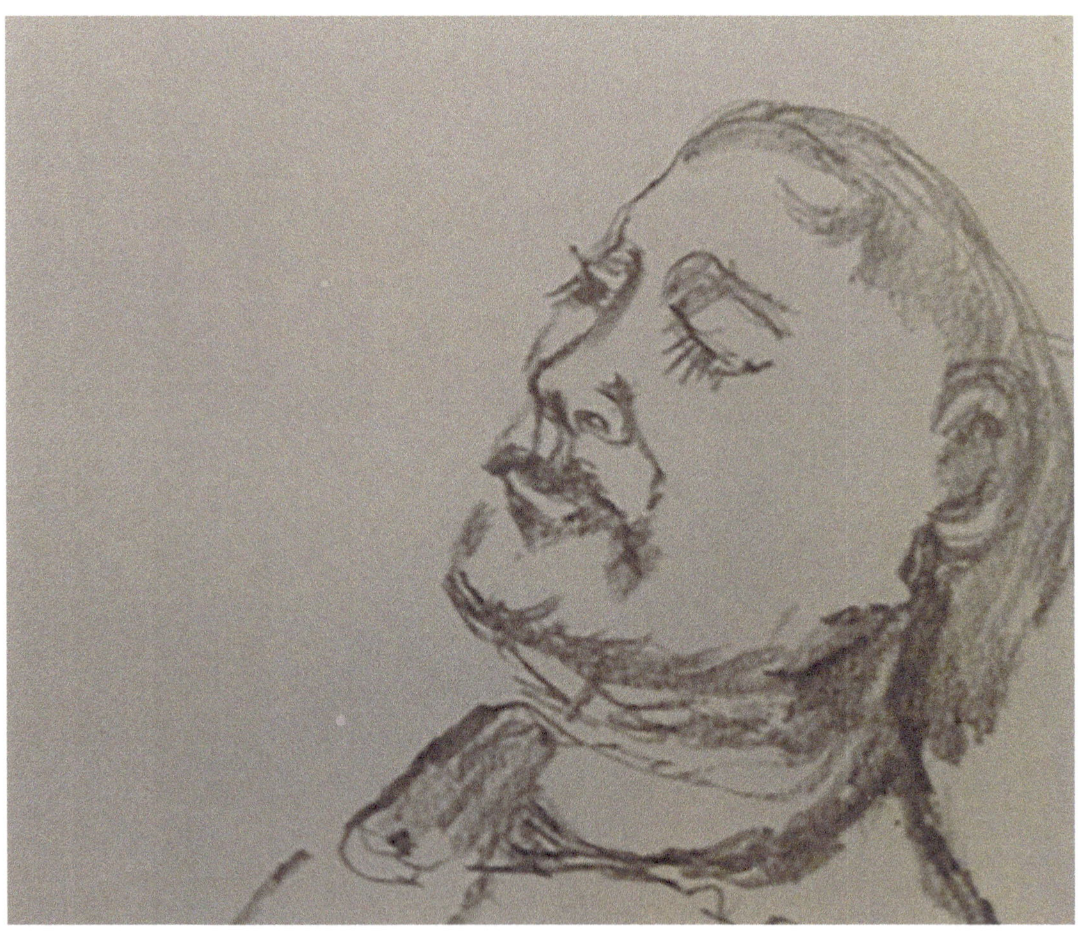

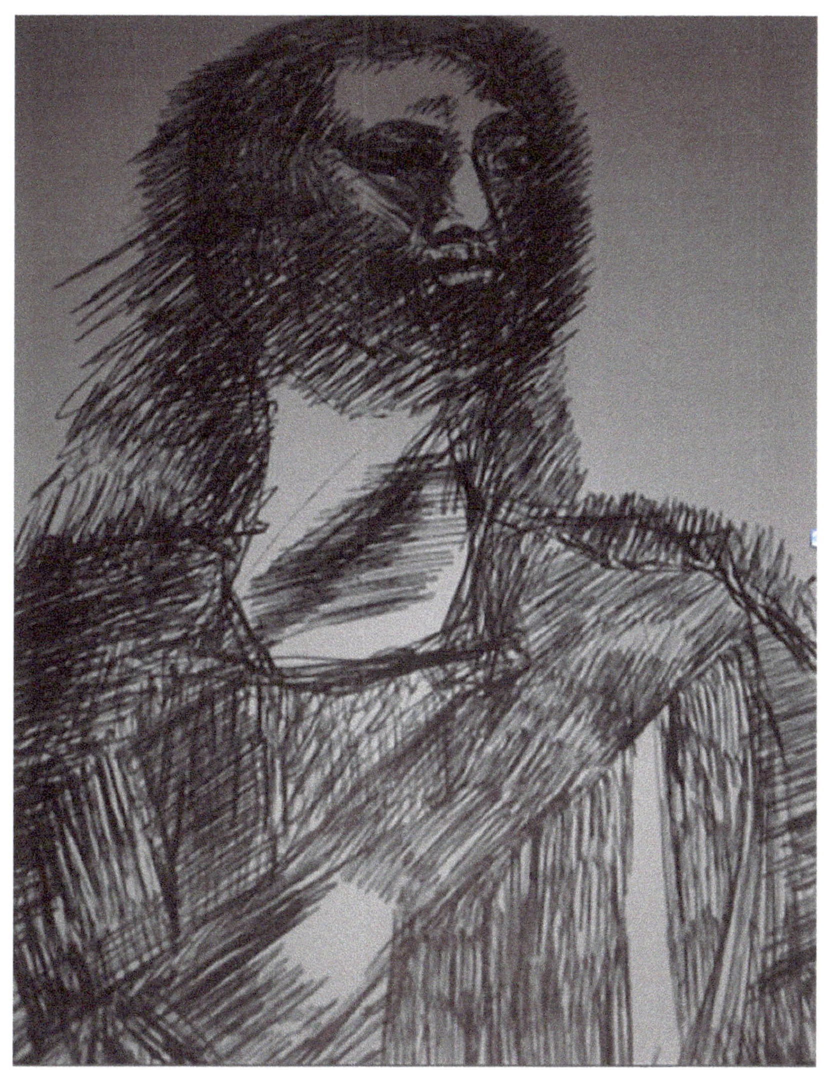

5. Darkened Prophet

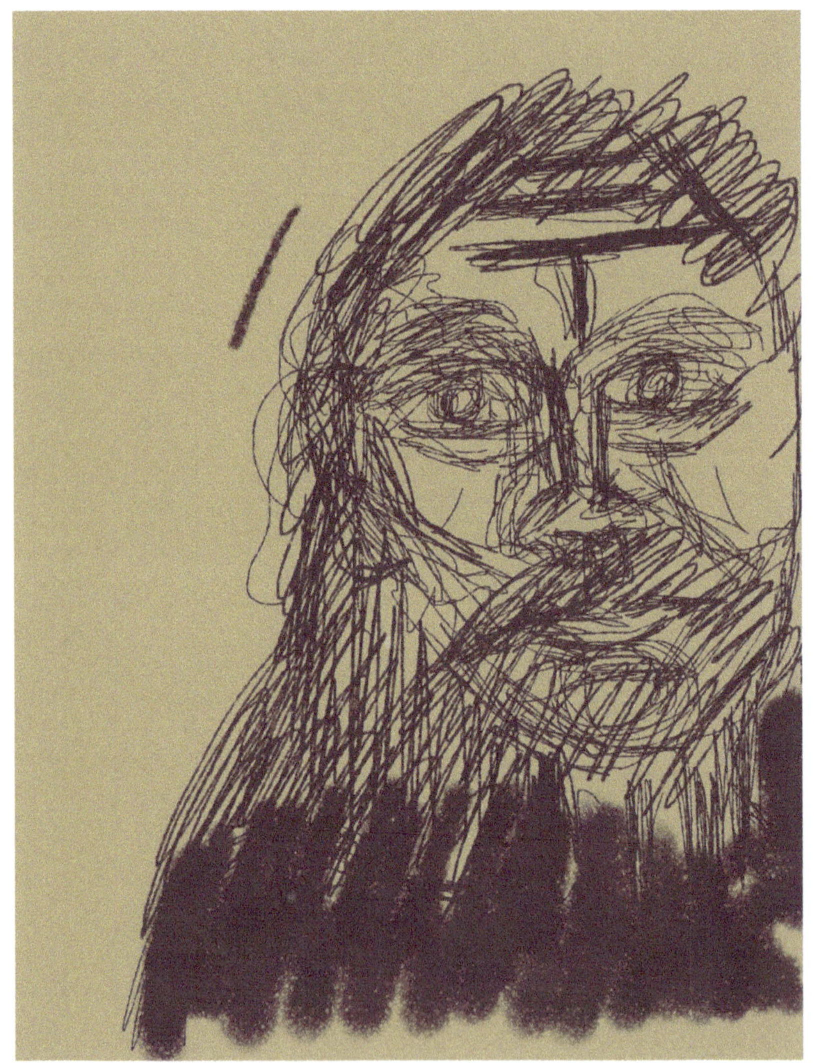

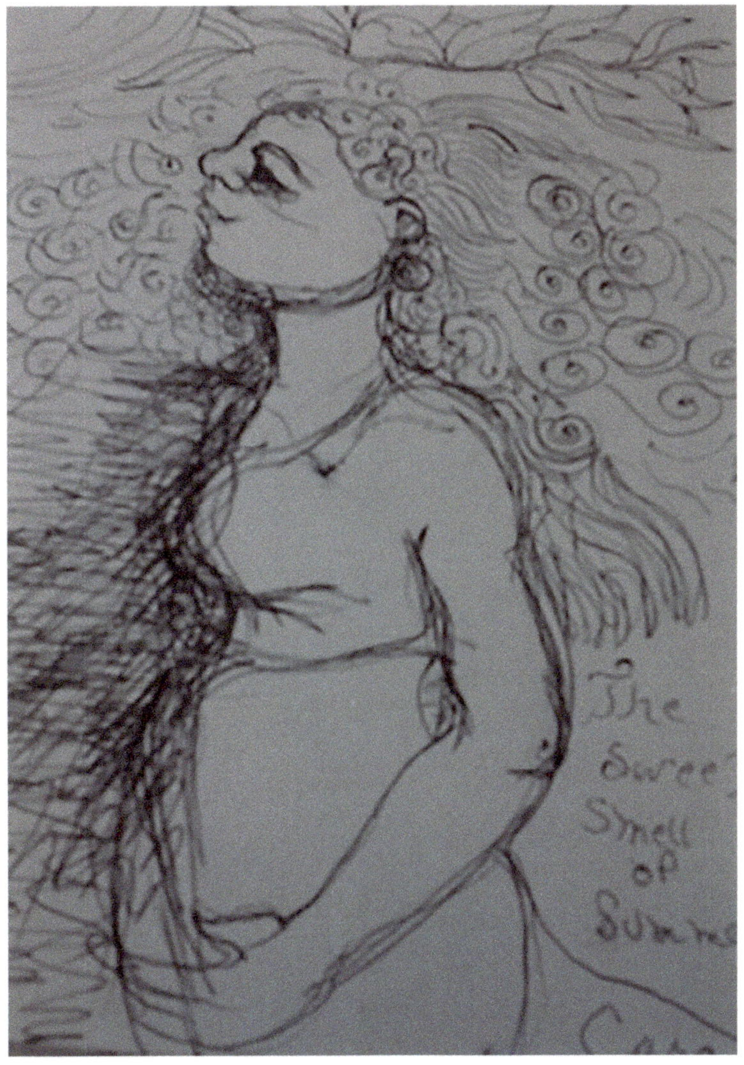

The
Swee
Smell
of
Summe

7. Portrait of a Fragment of a Man

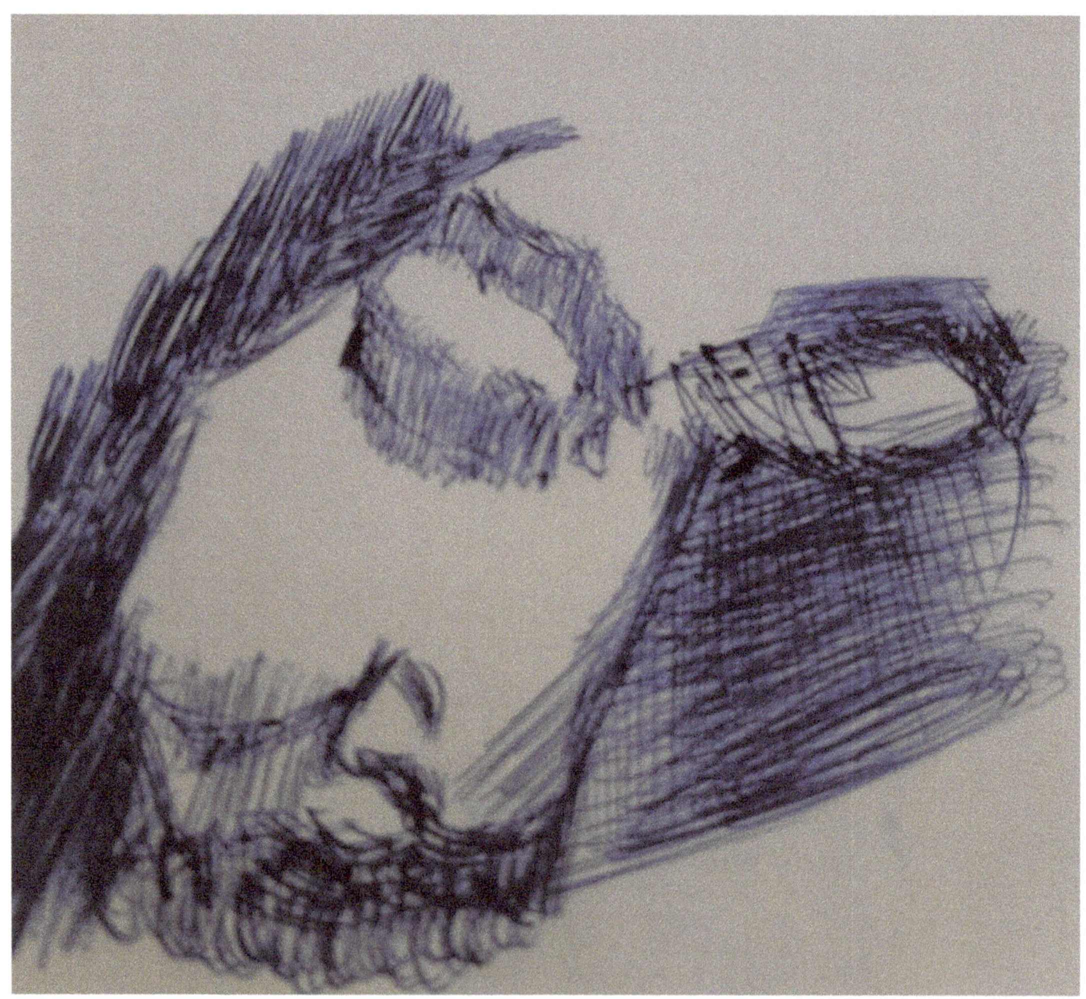

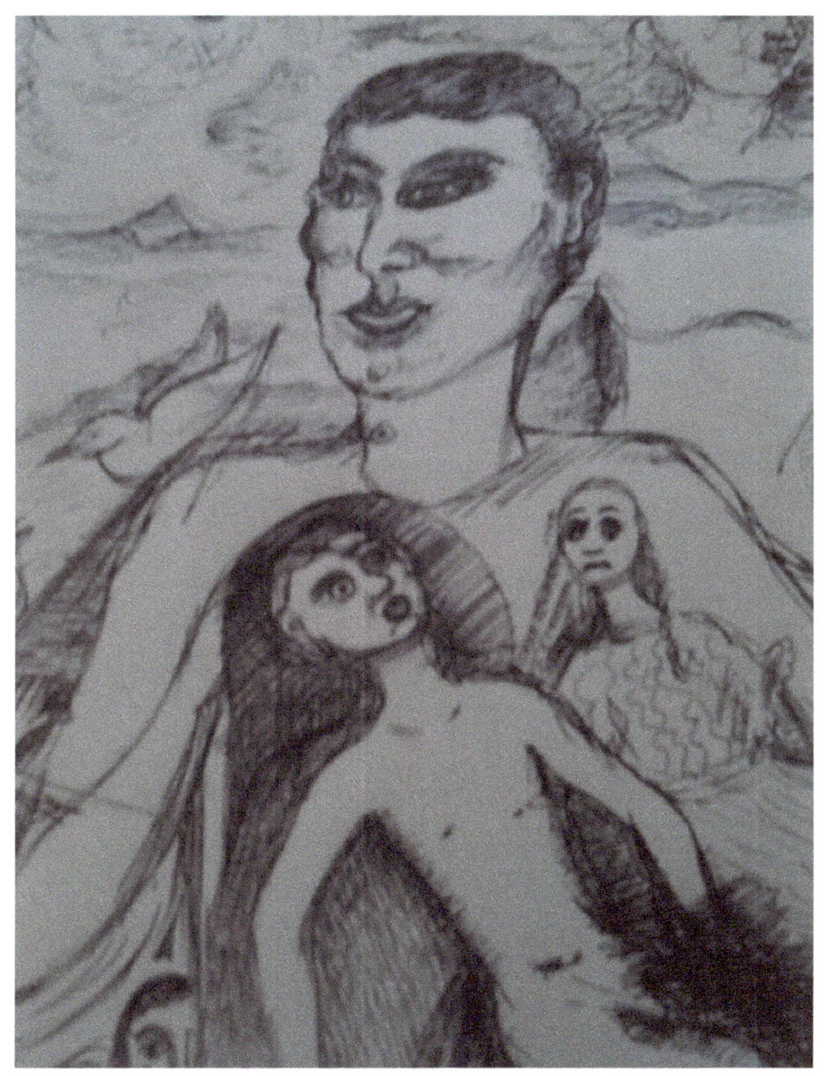

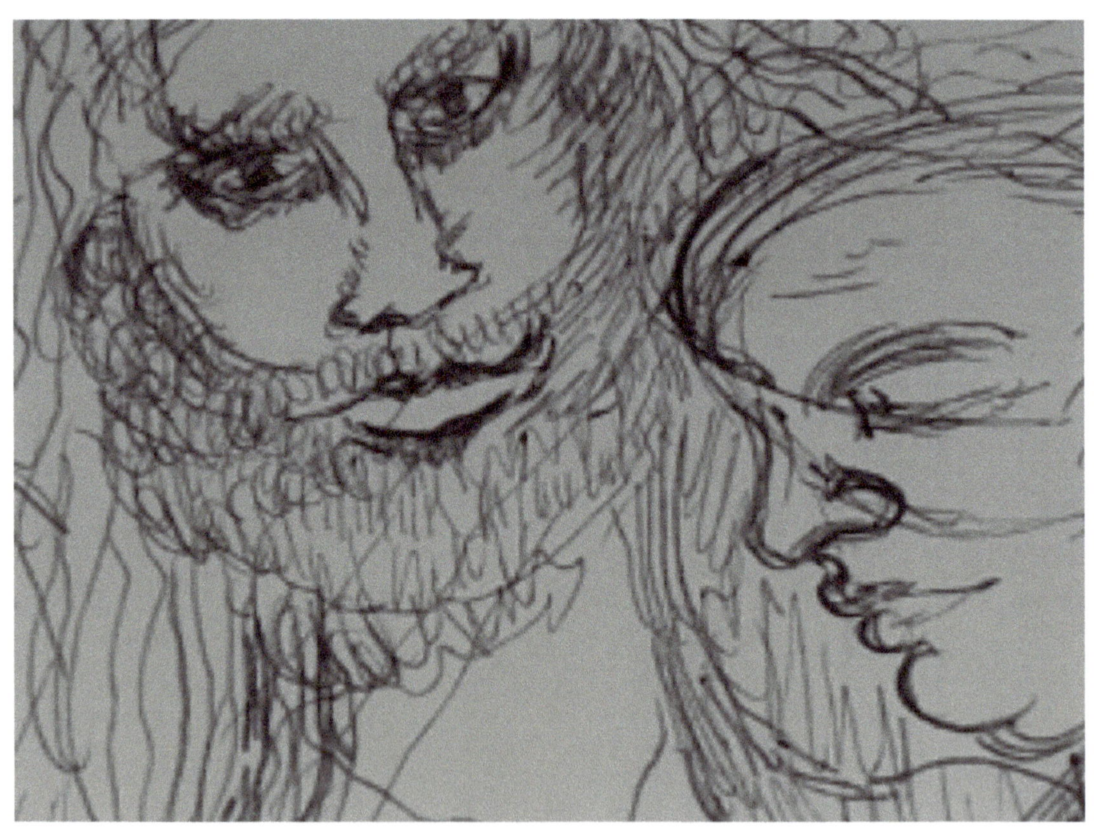

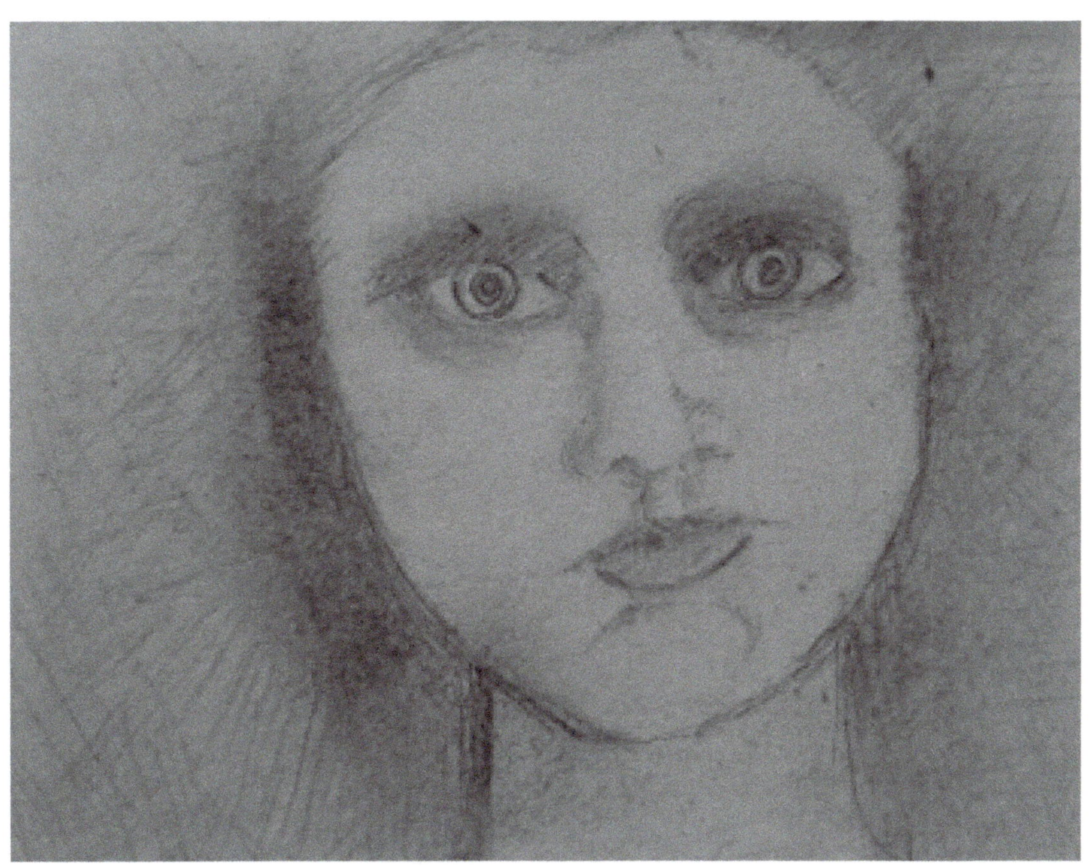

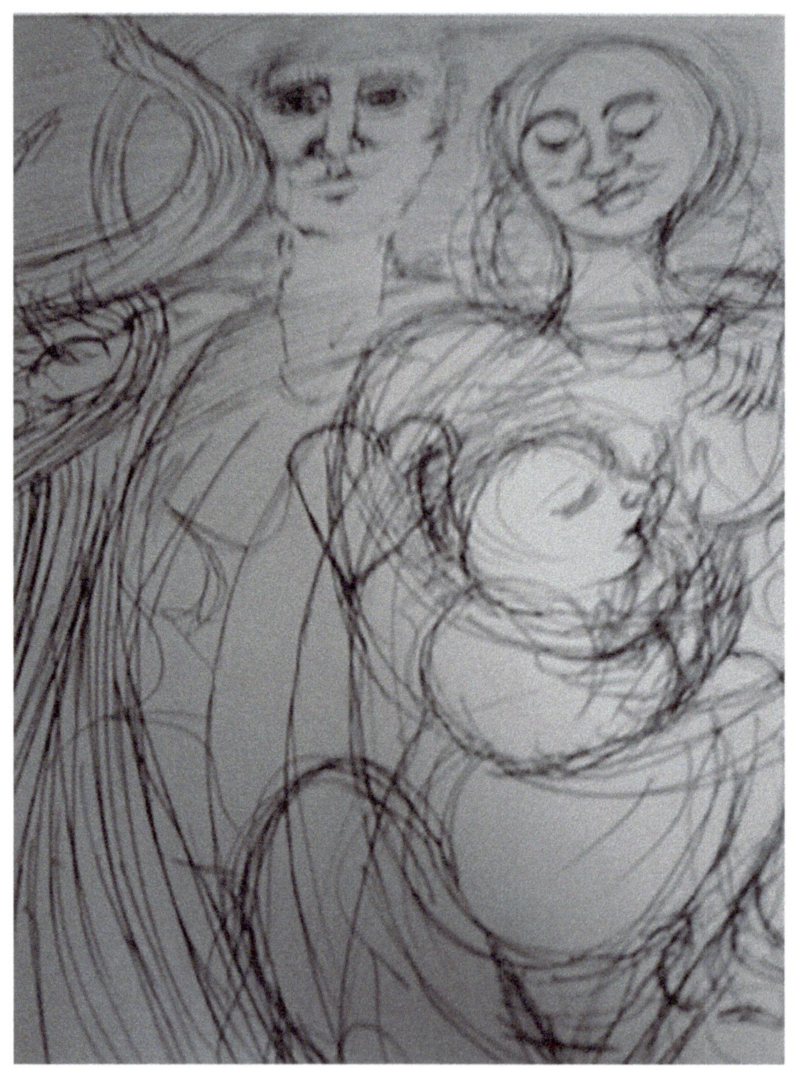

12. Labyrinth Dream

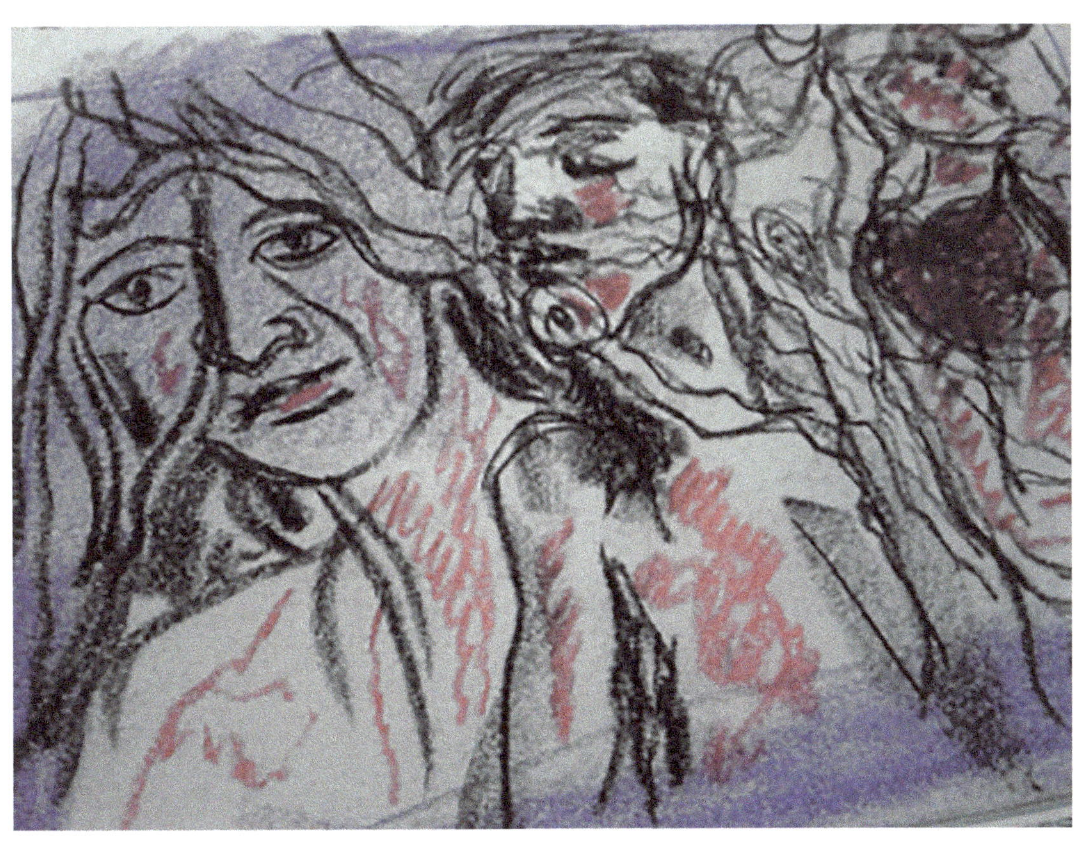

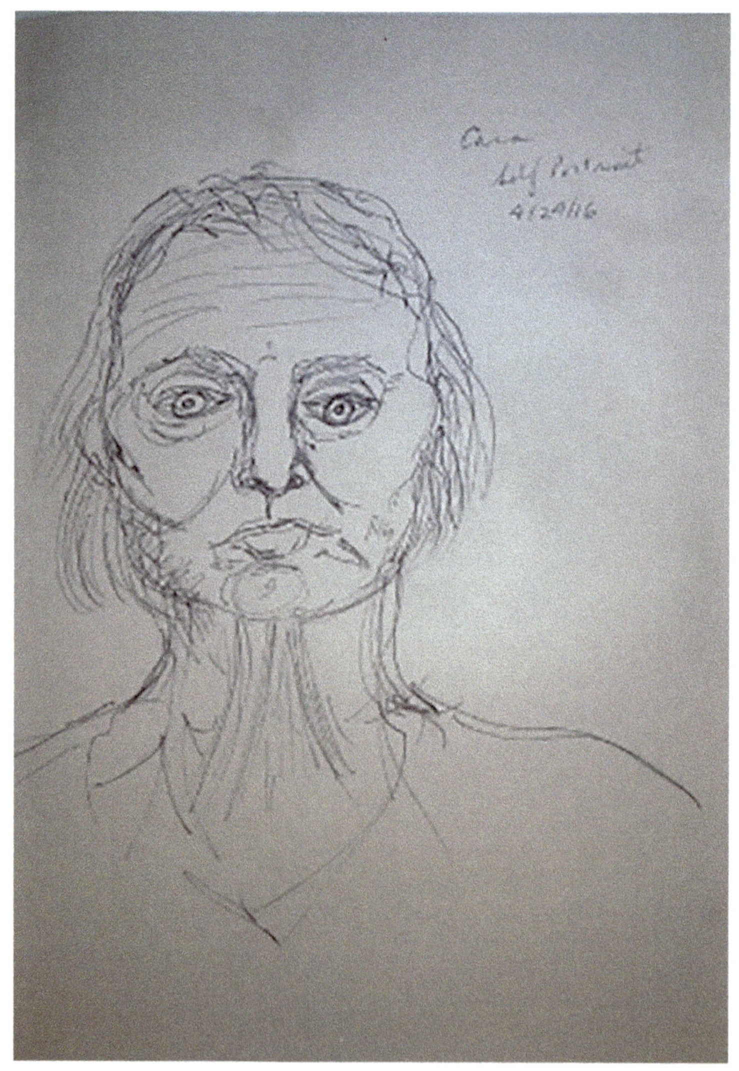

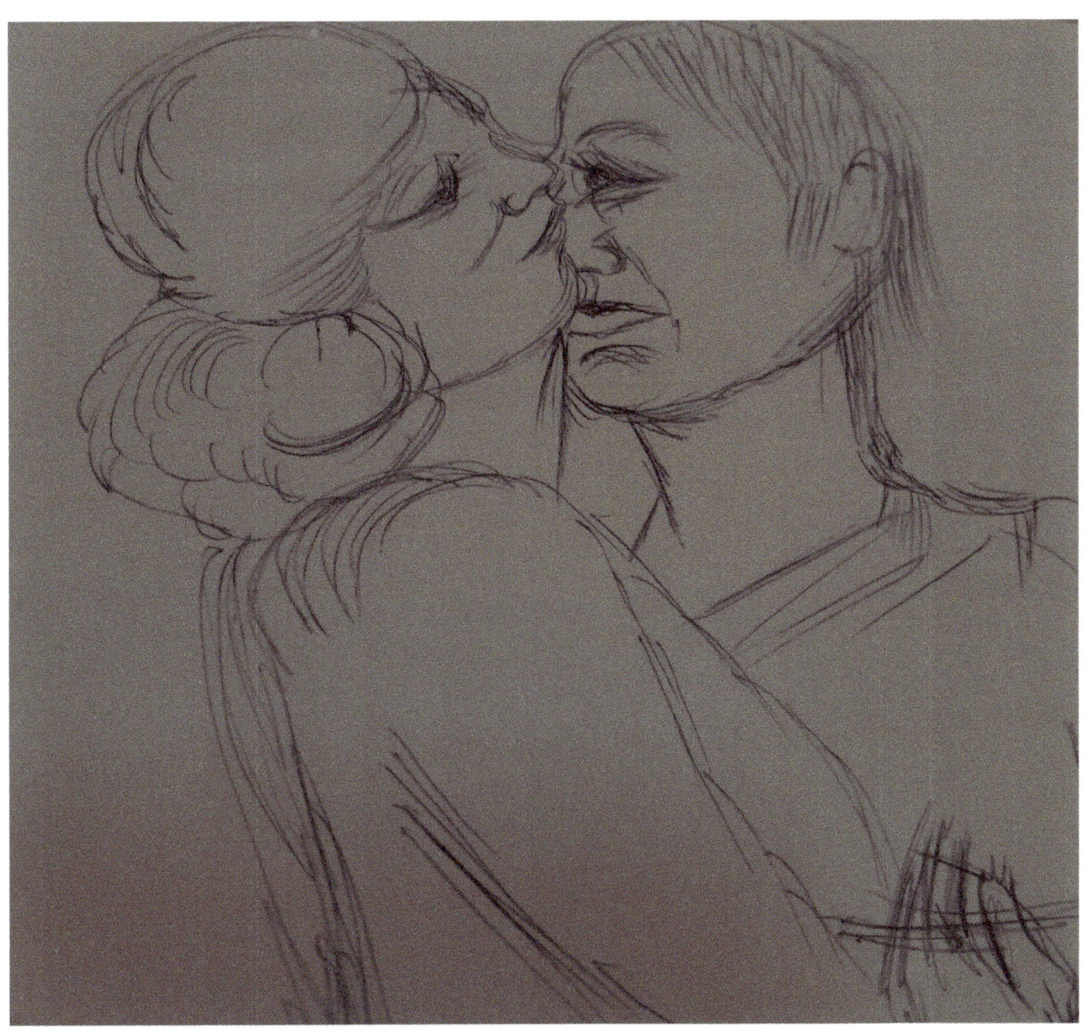

15. Befriending Women

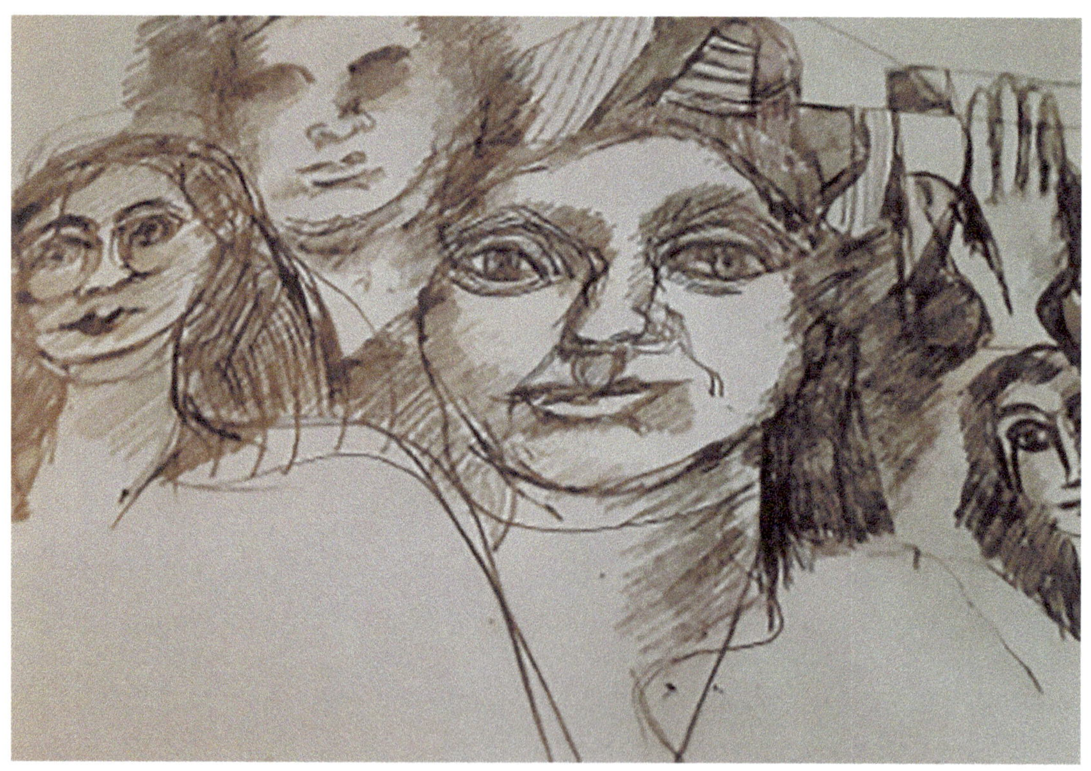

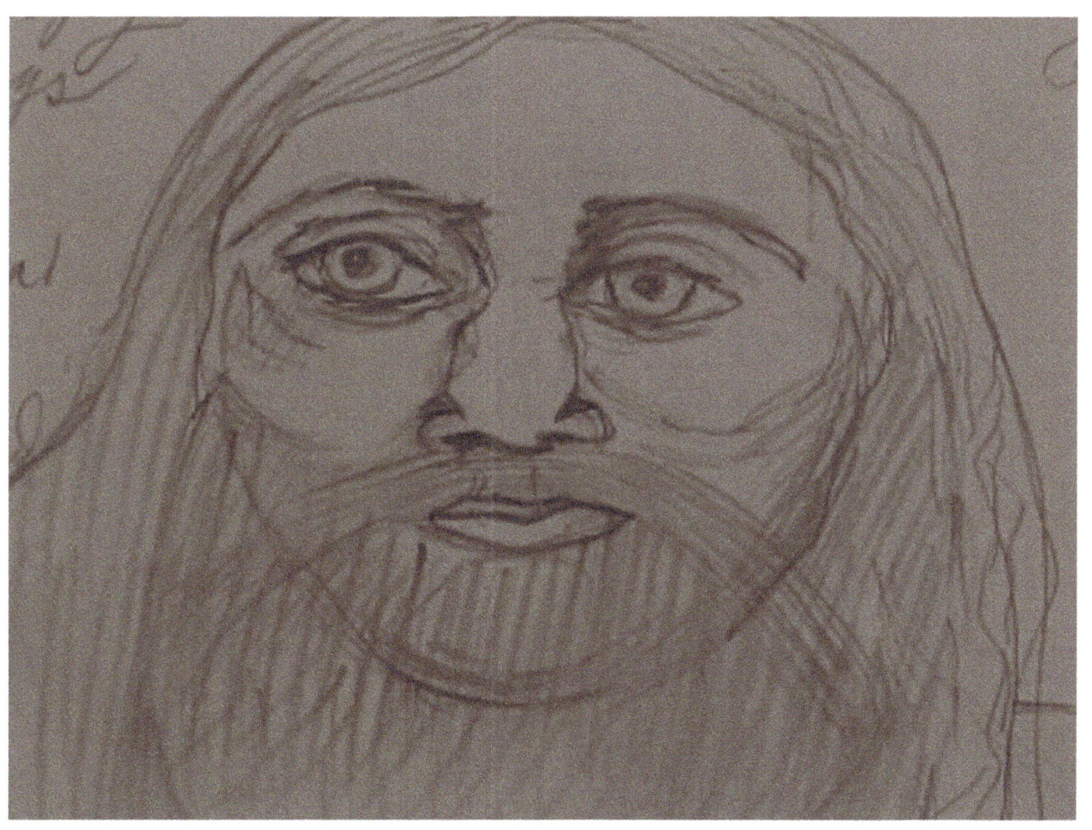

16. The Lord in Prayer

17. Self-Portrait

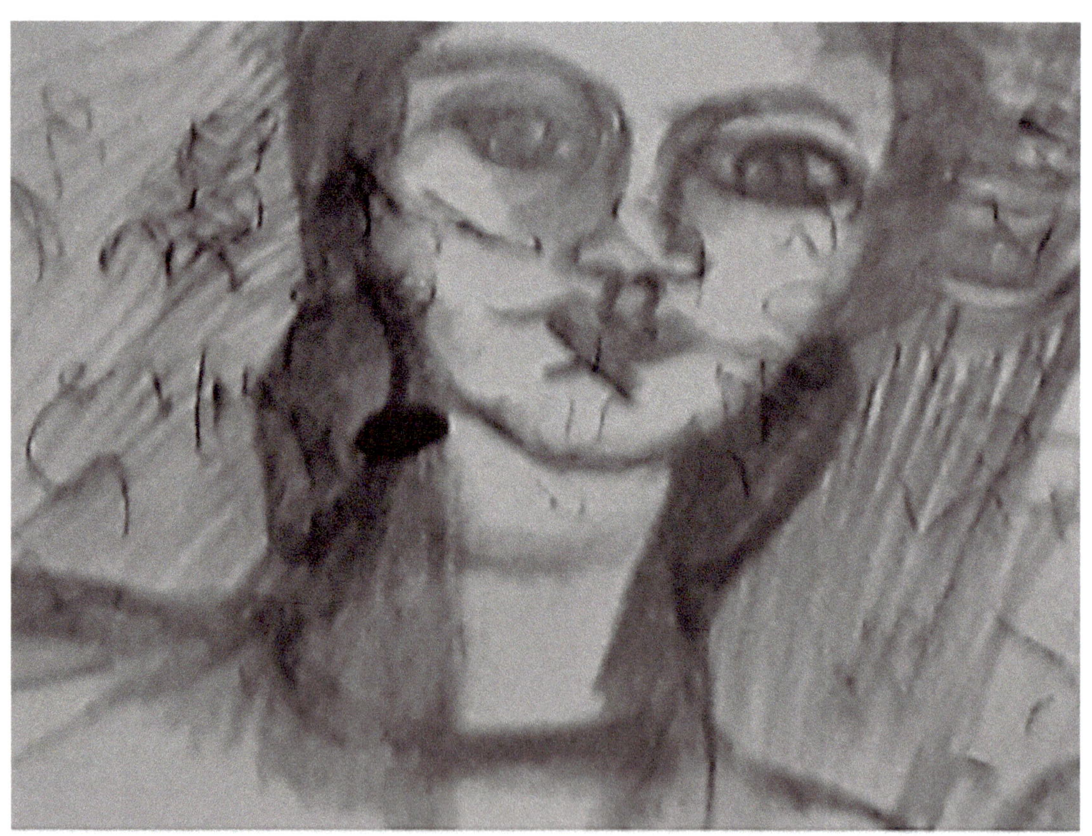

32

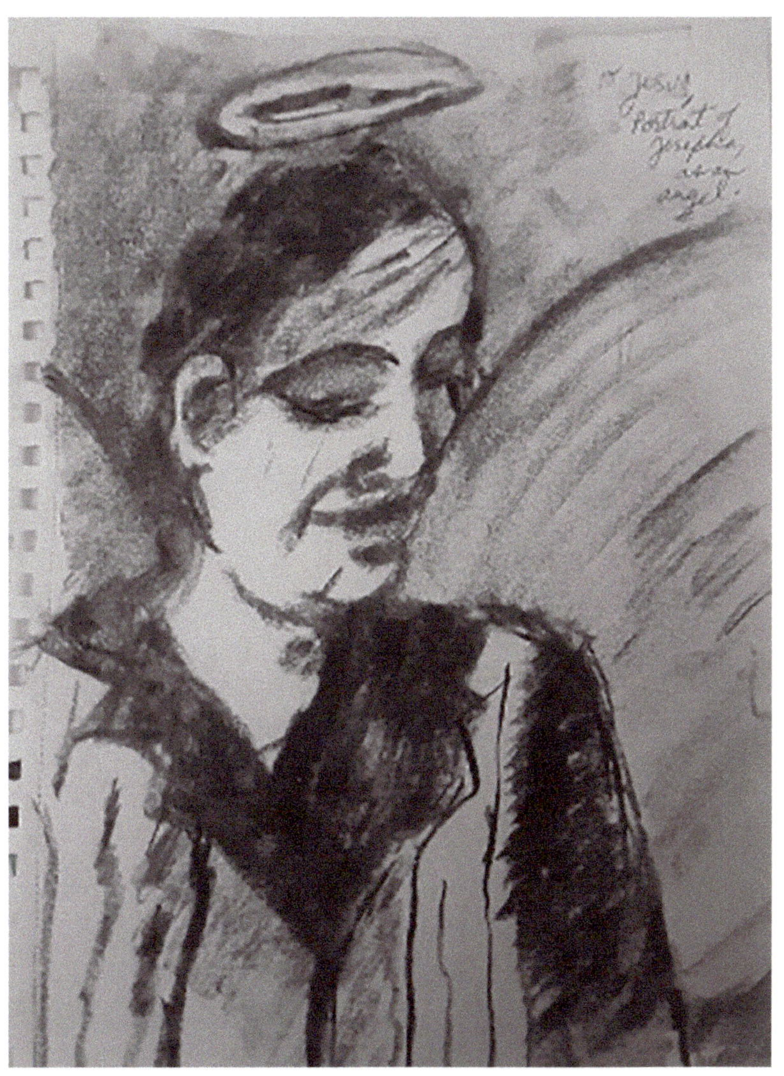

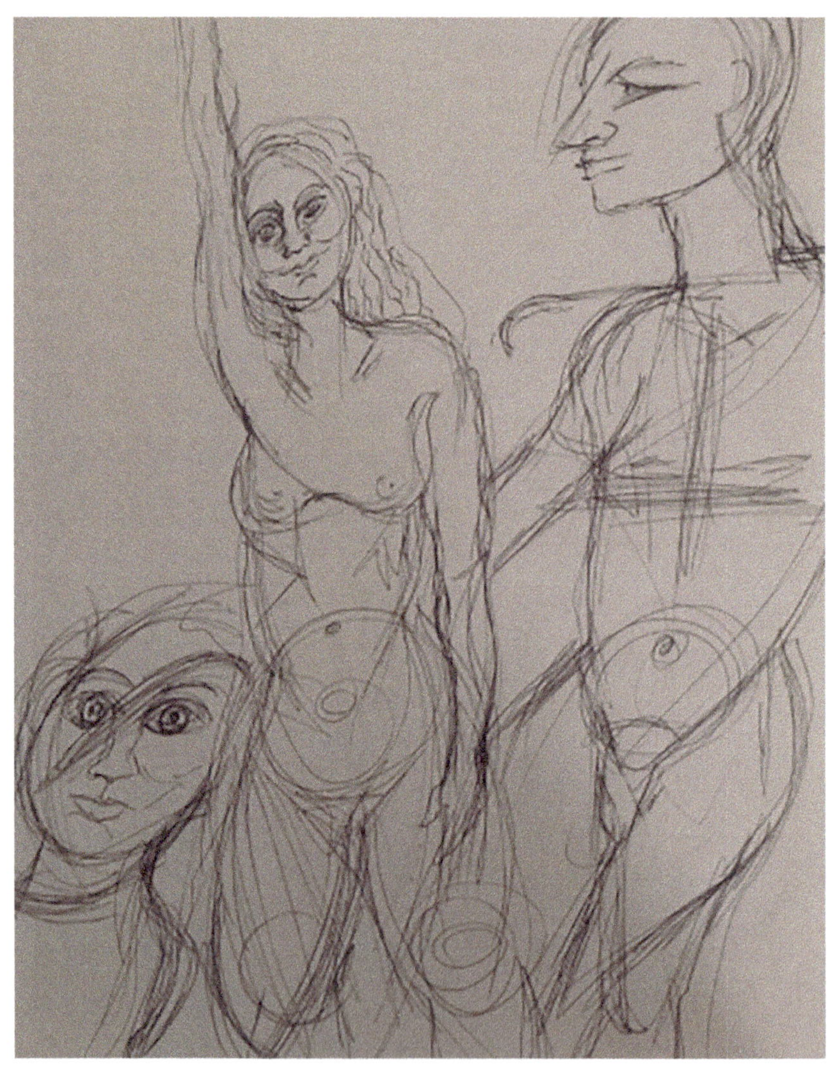

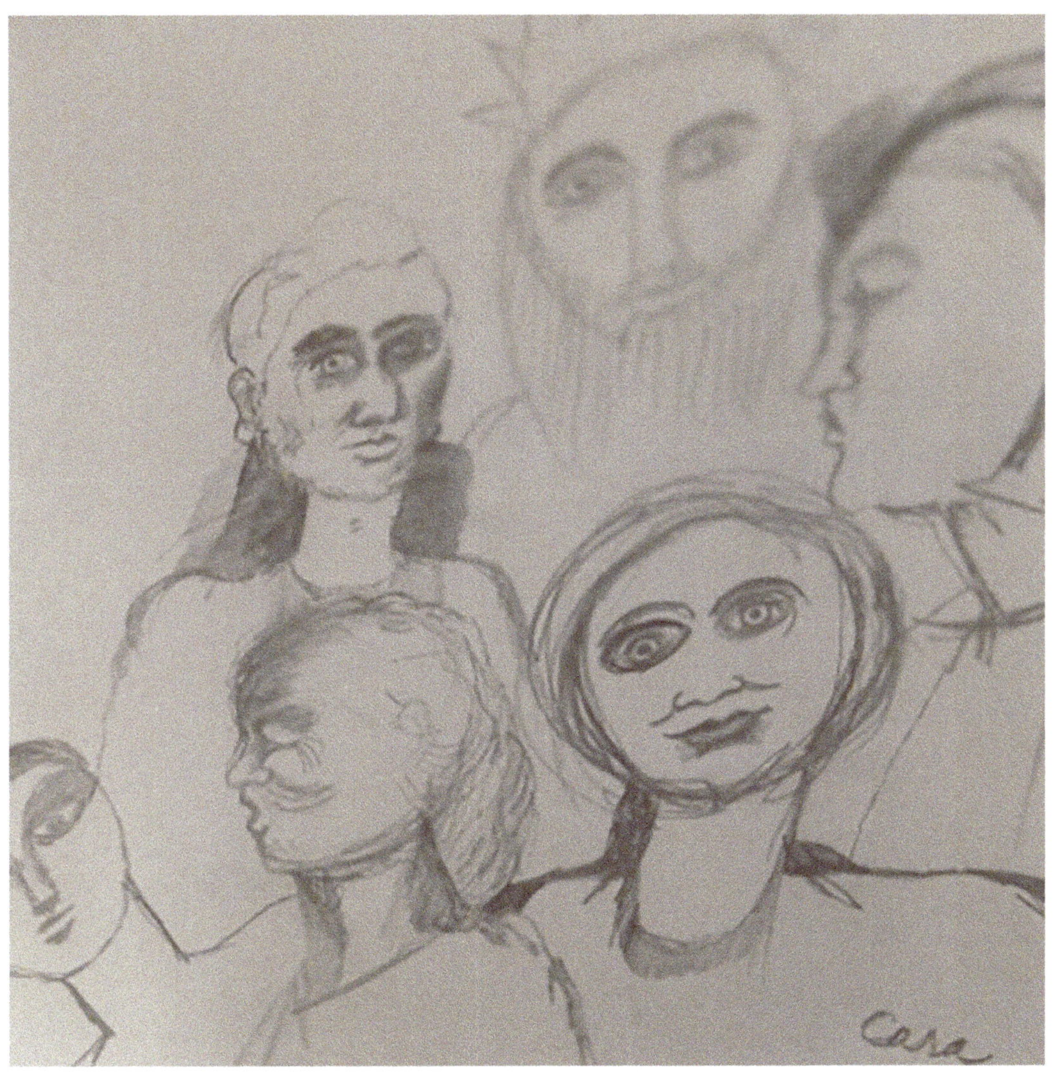

21. Come Closer to Me

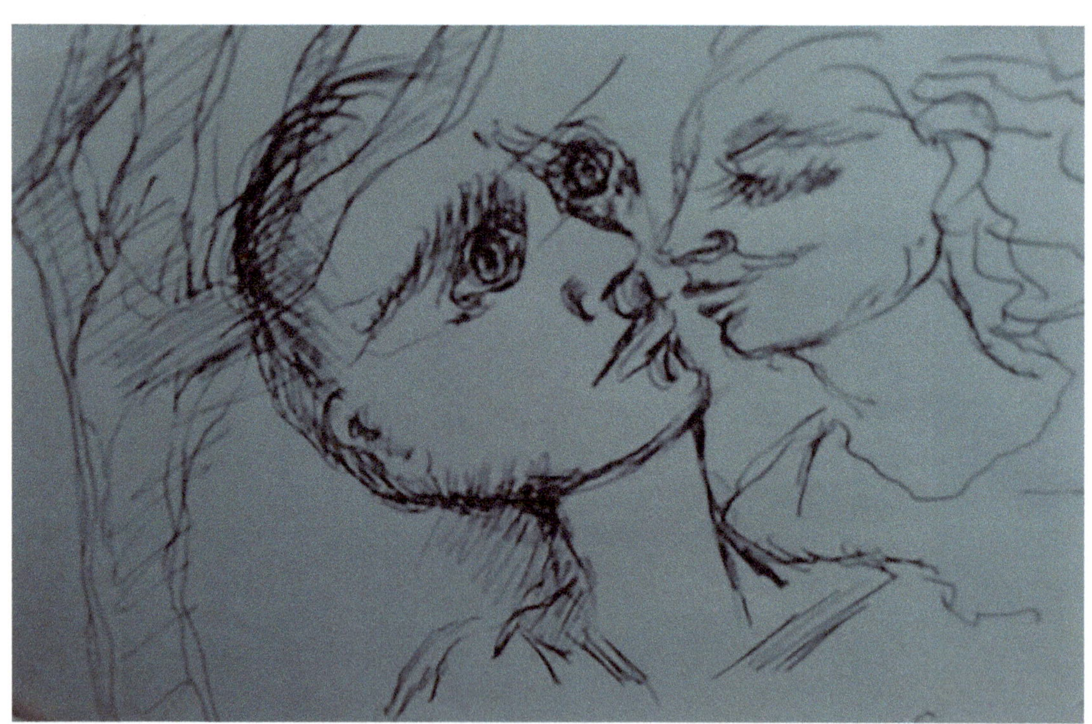

36

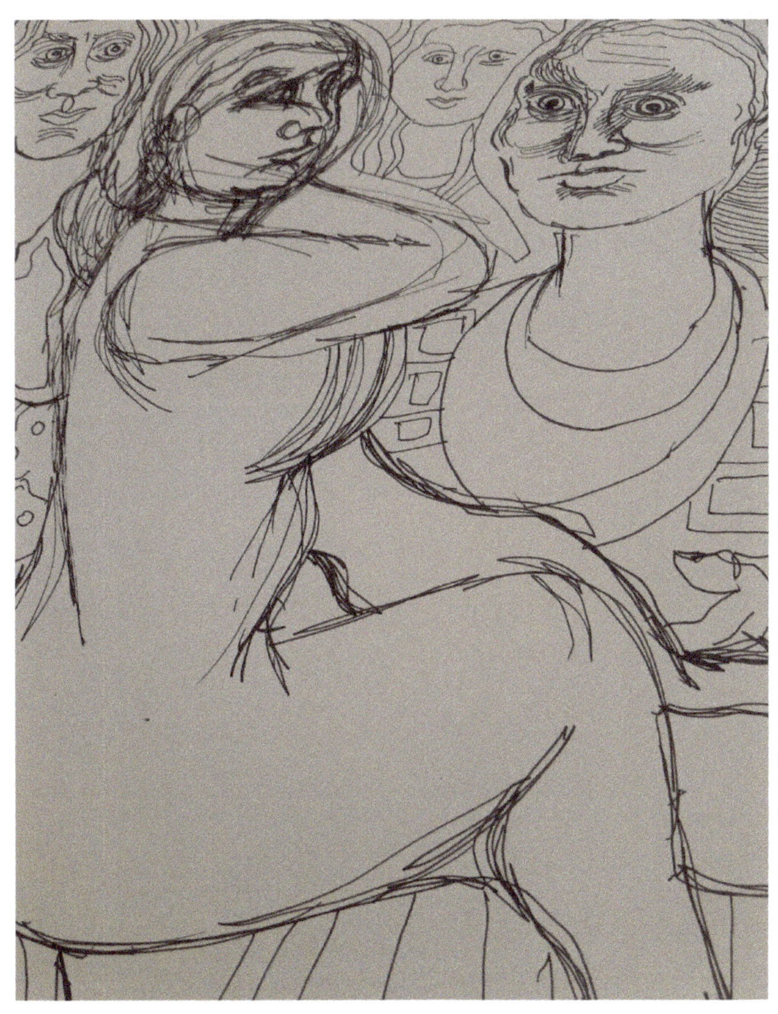

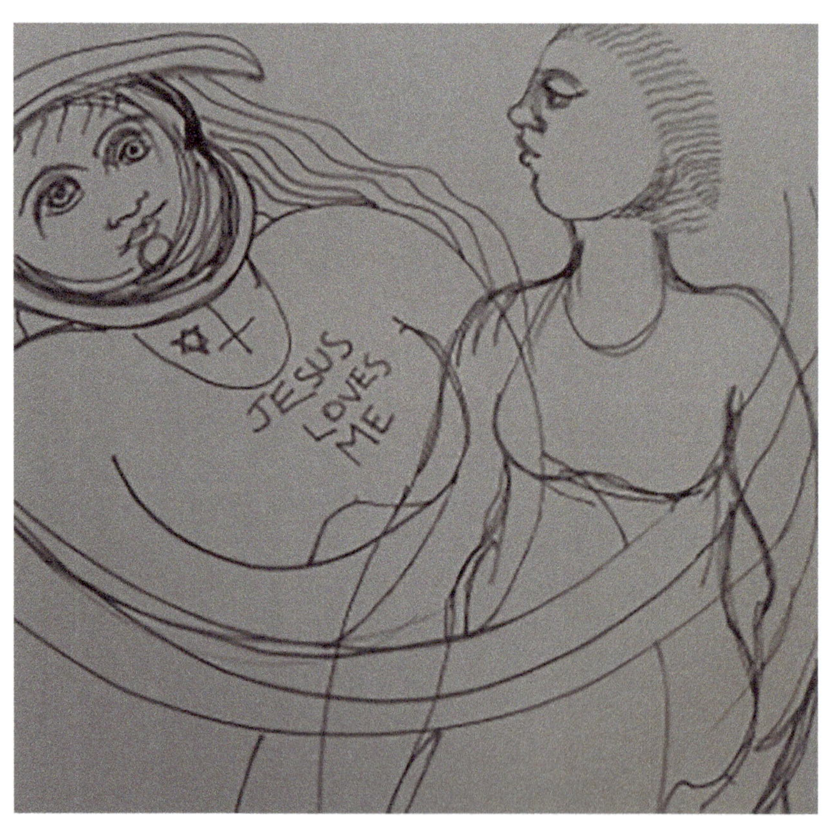

JESUS
LOVES
ME

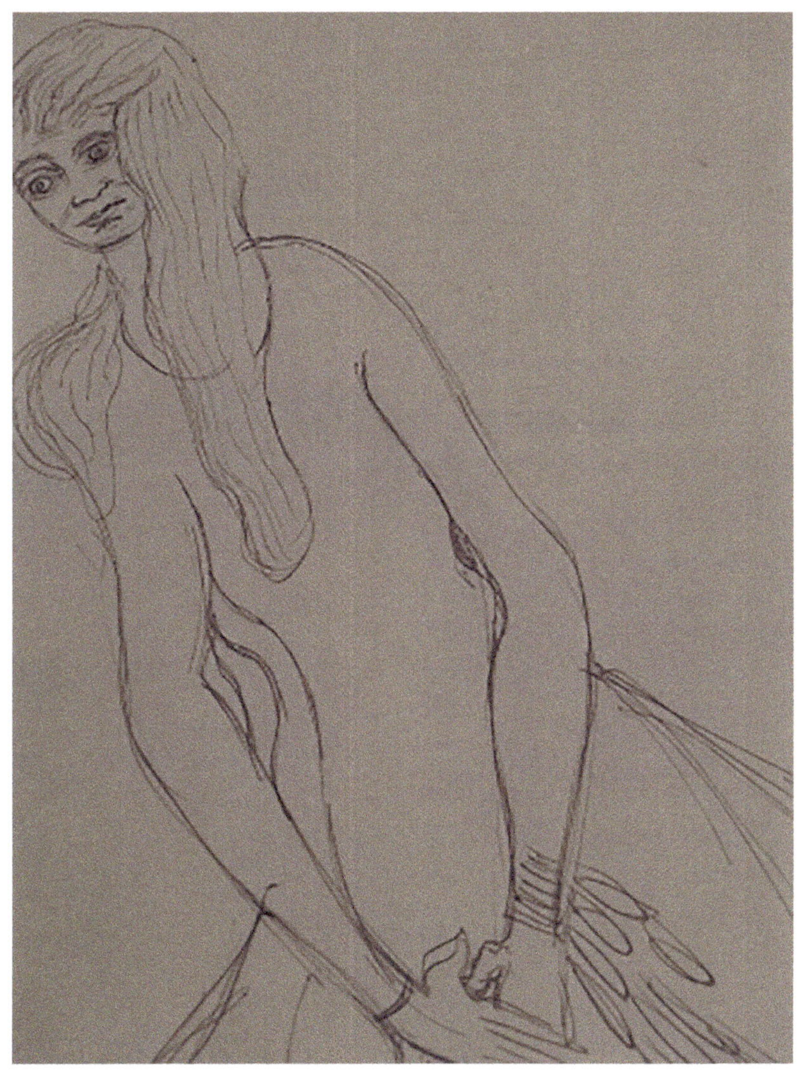

25. Seeking God

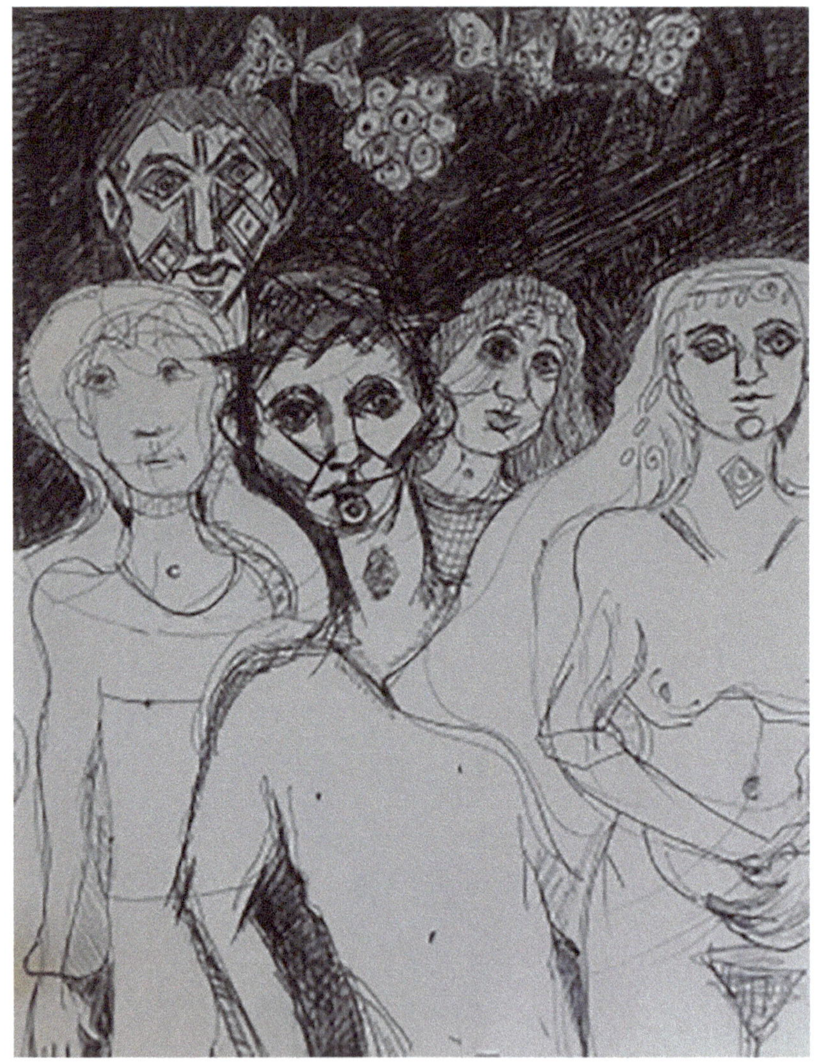

40

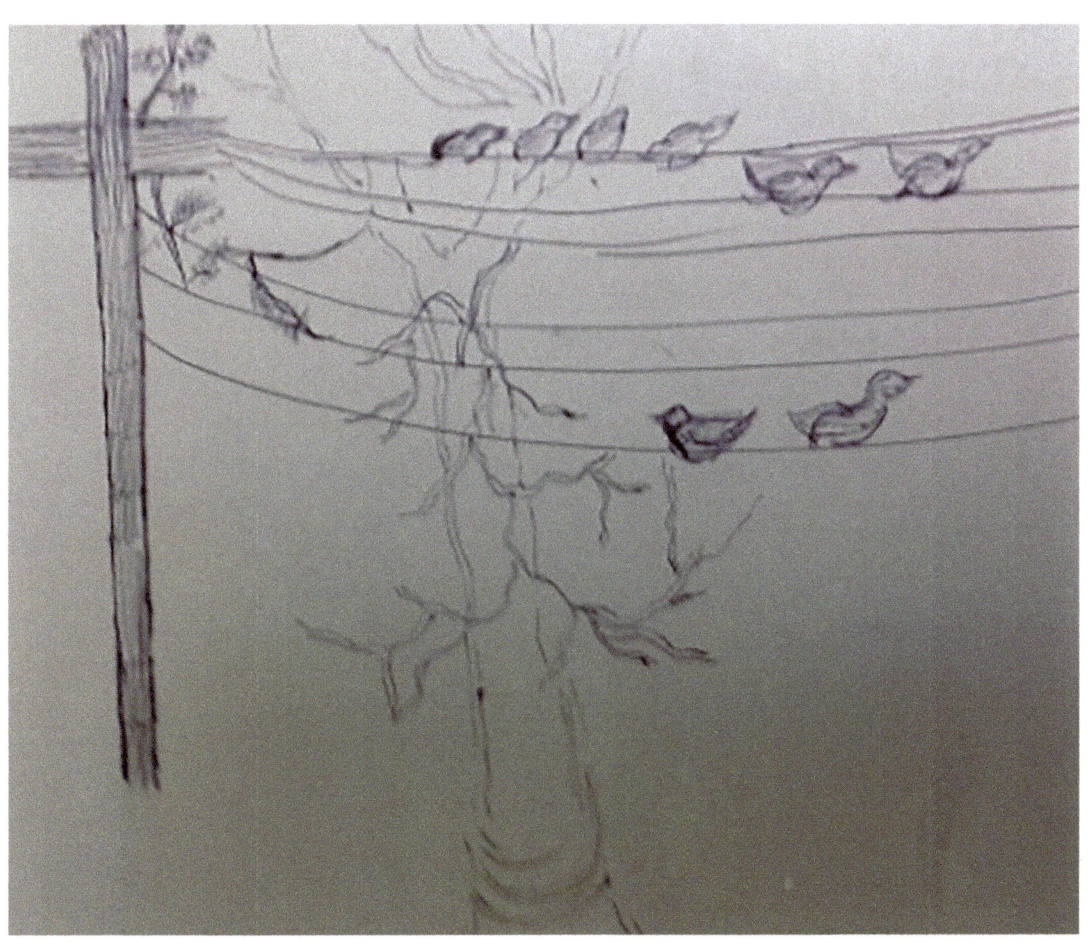

27. Adam and Eve

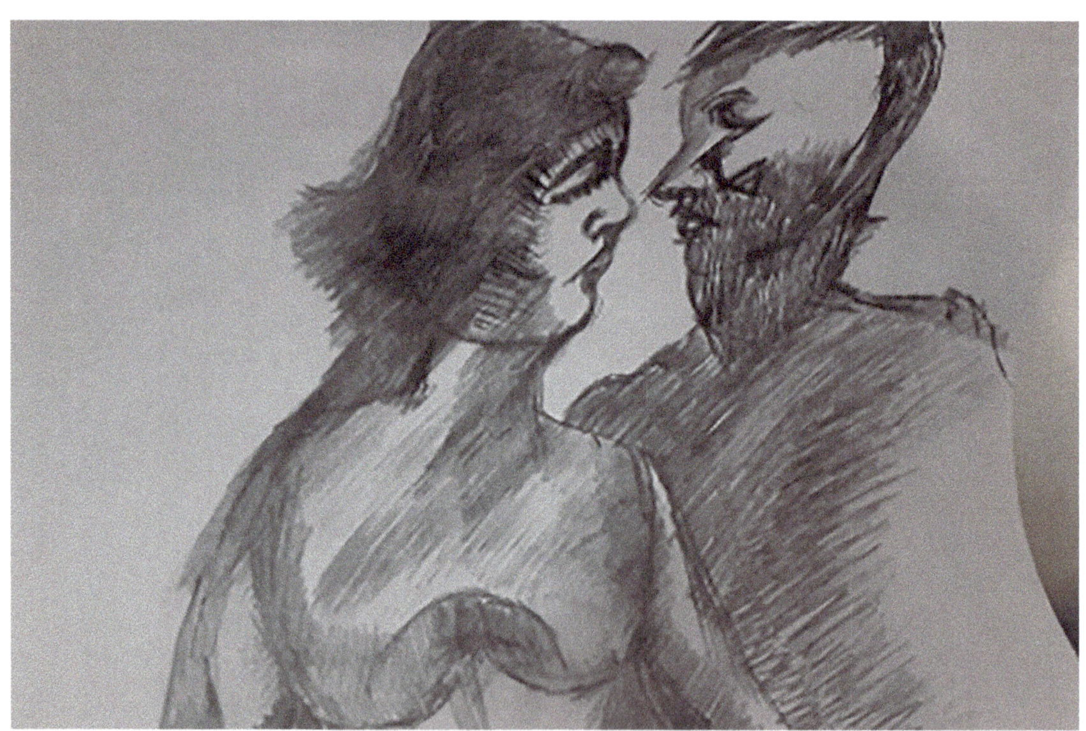

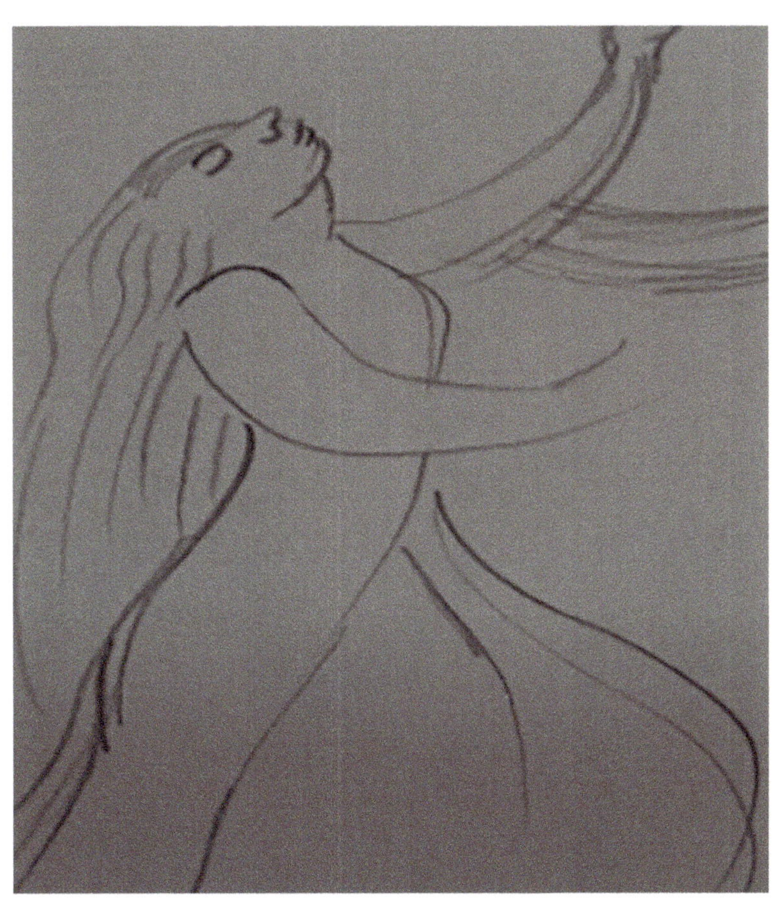

28. Dancer Glory

29. Angels Calling

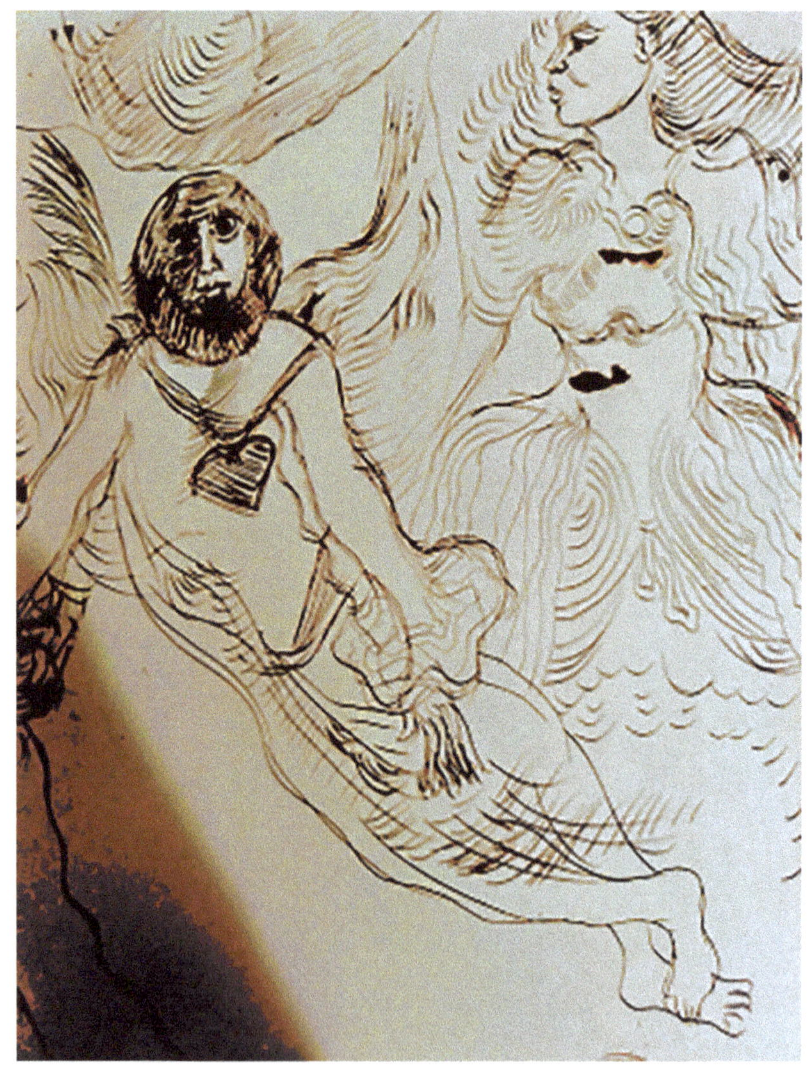

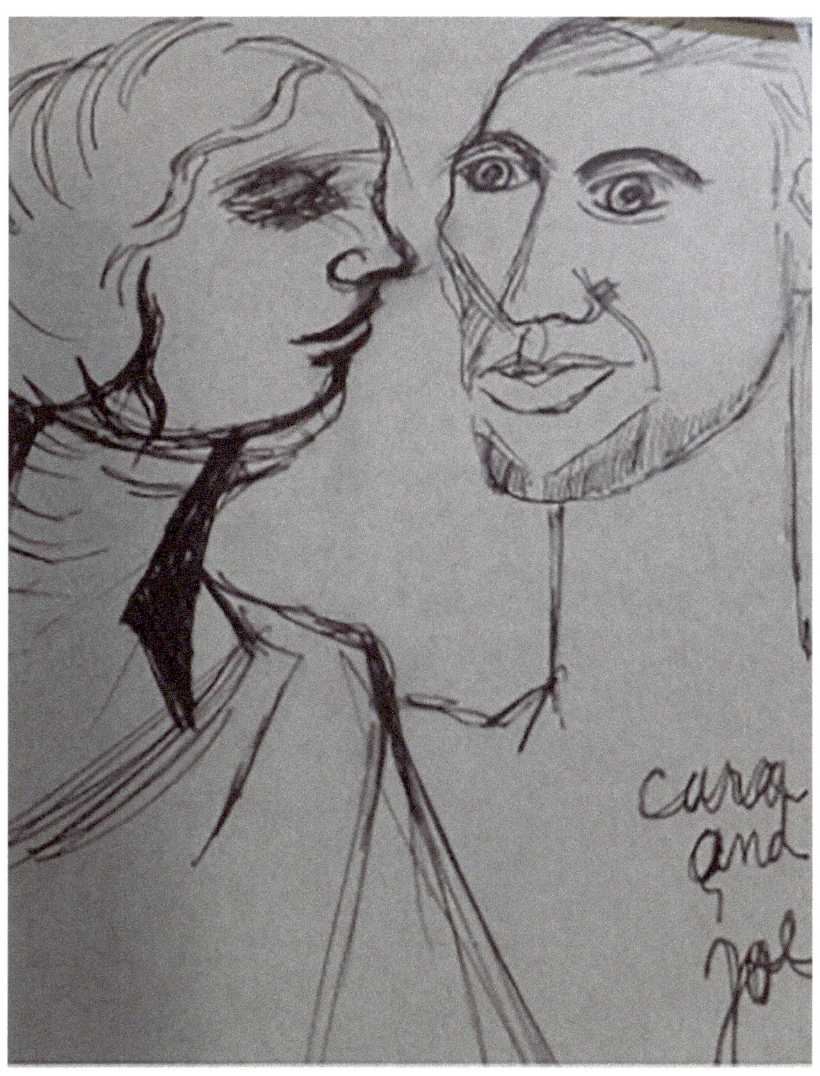

31. Joseph, You Are My Beloved

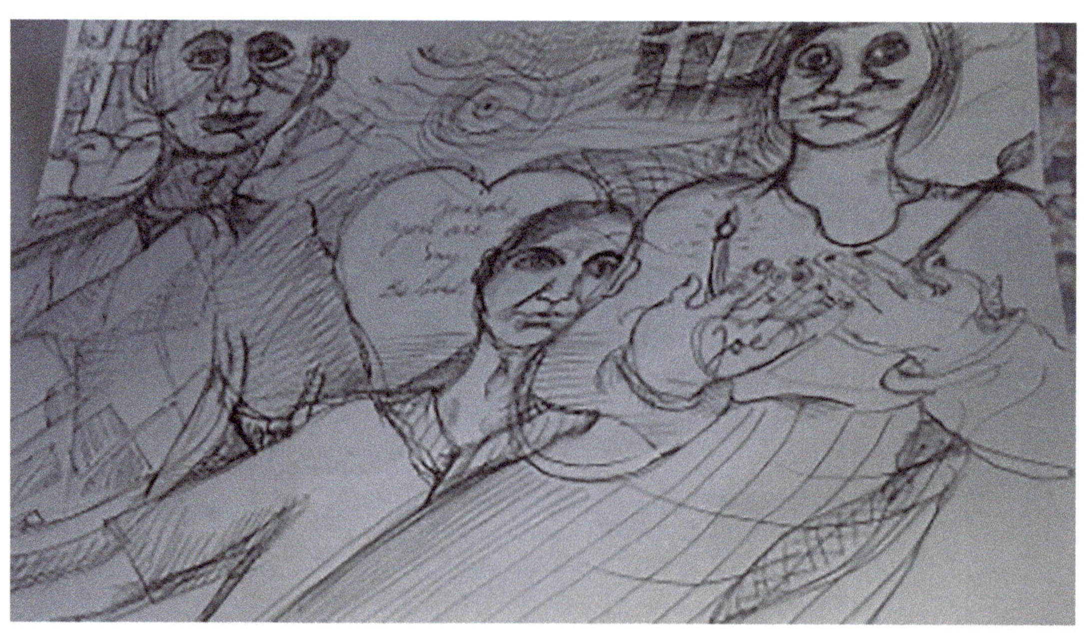

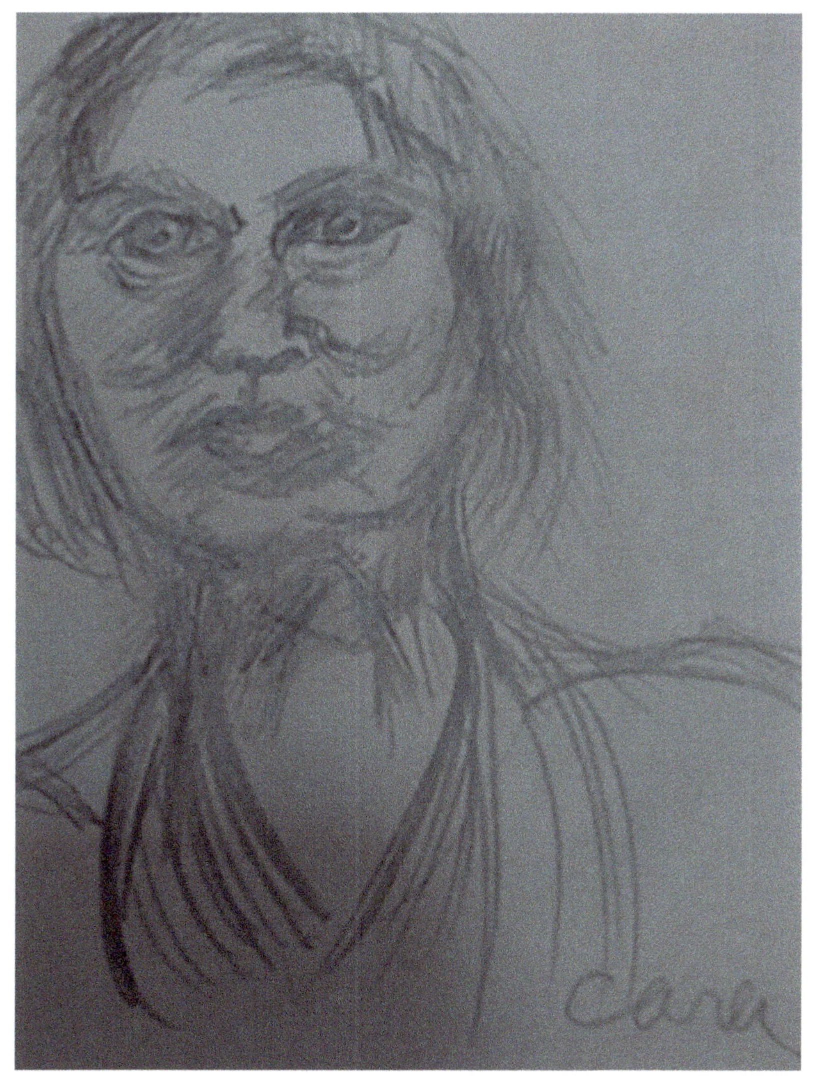

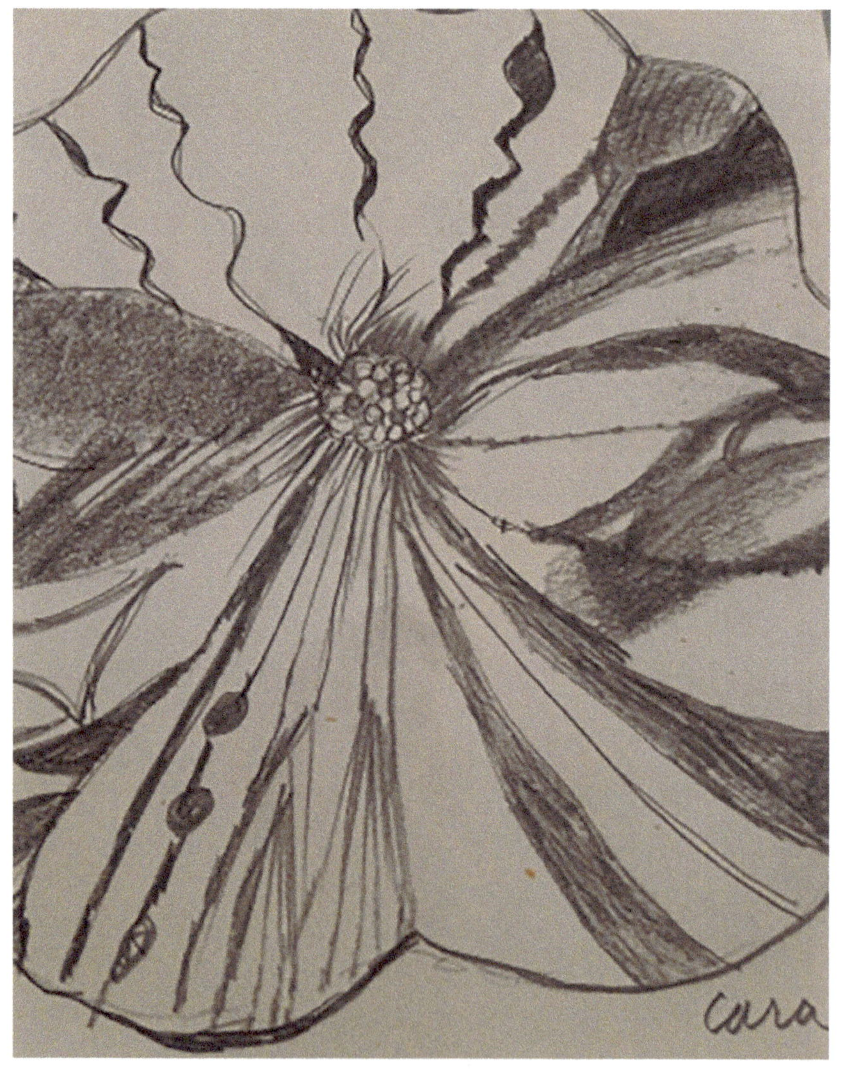

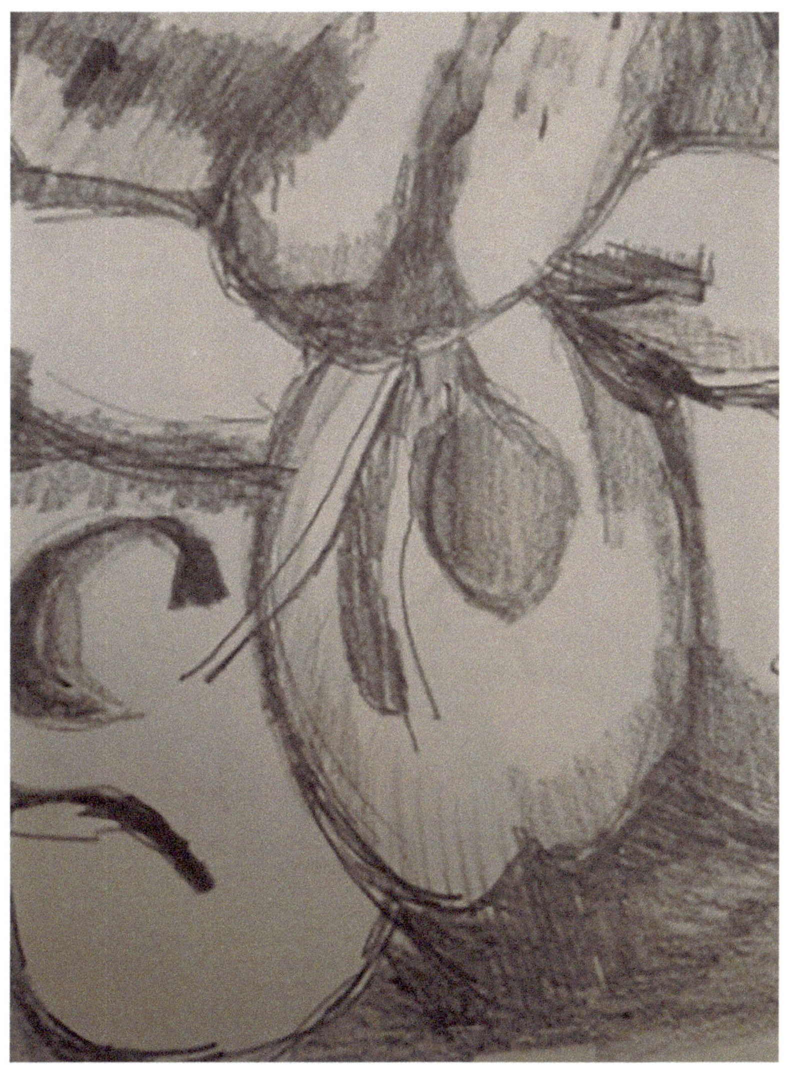

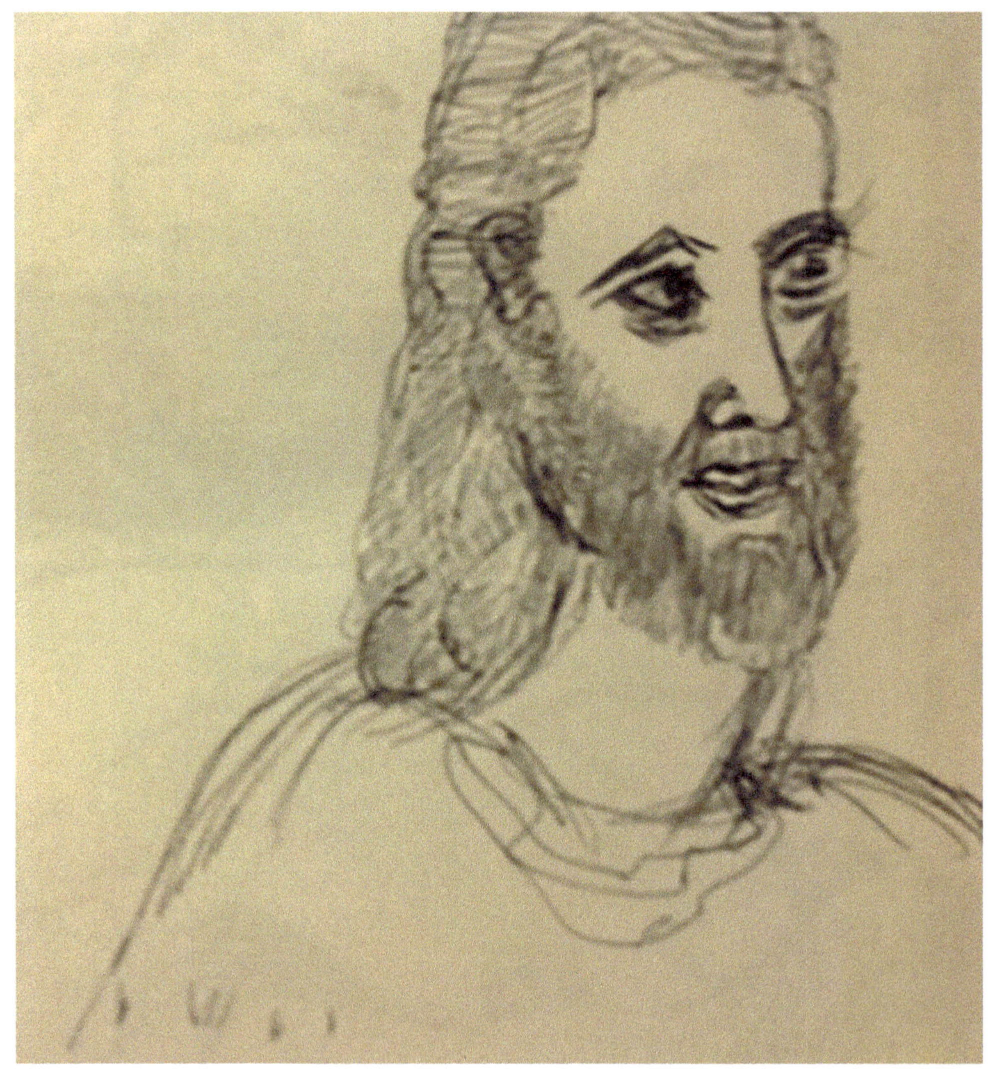

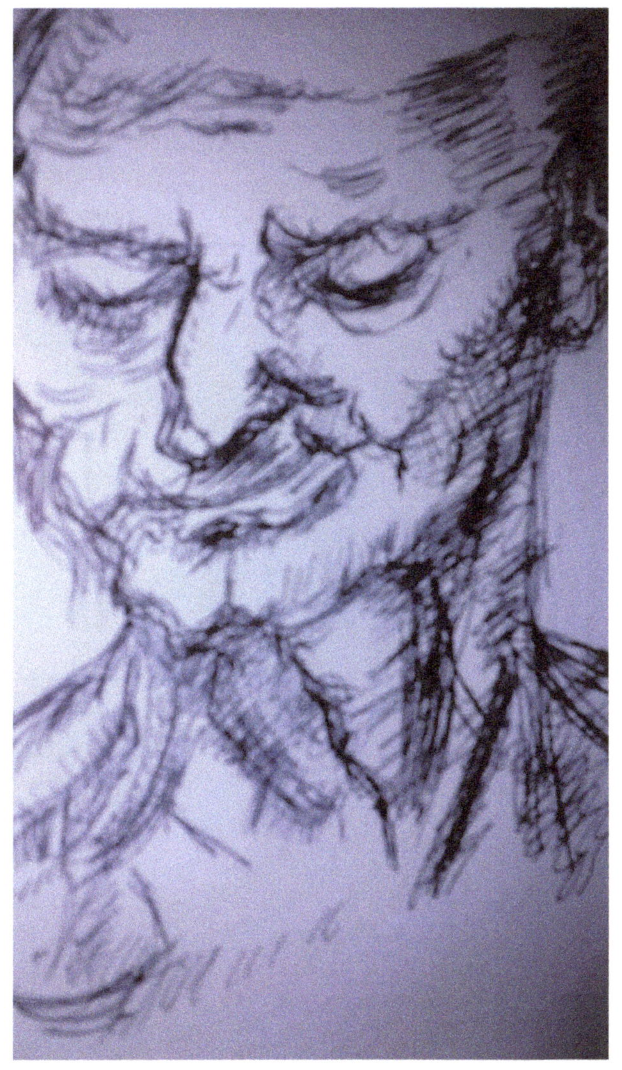

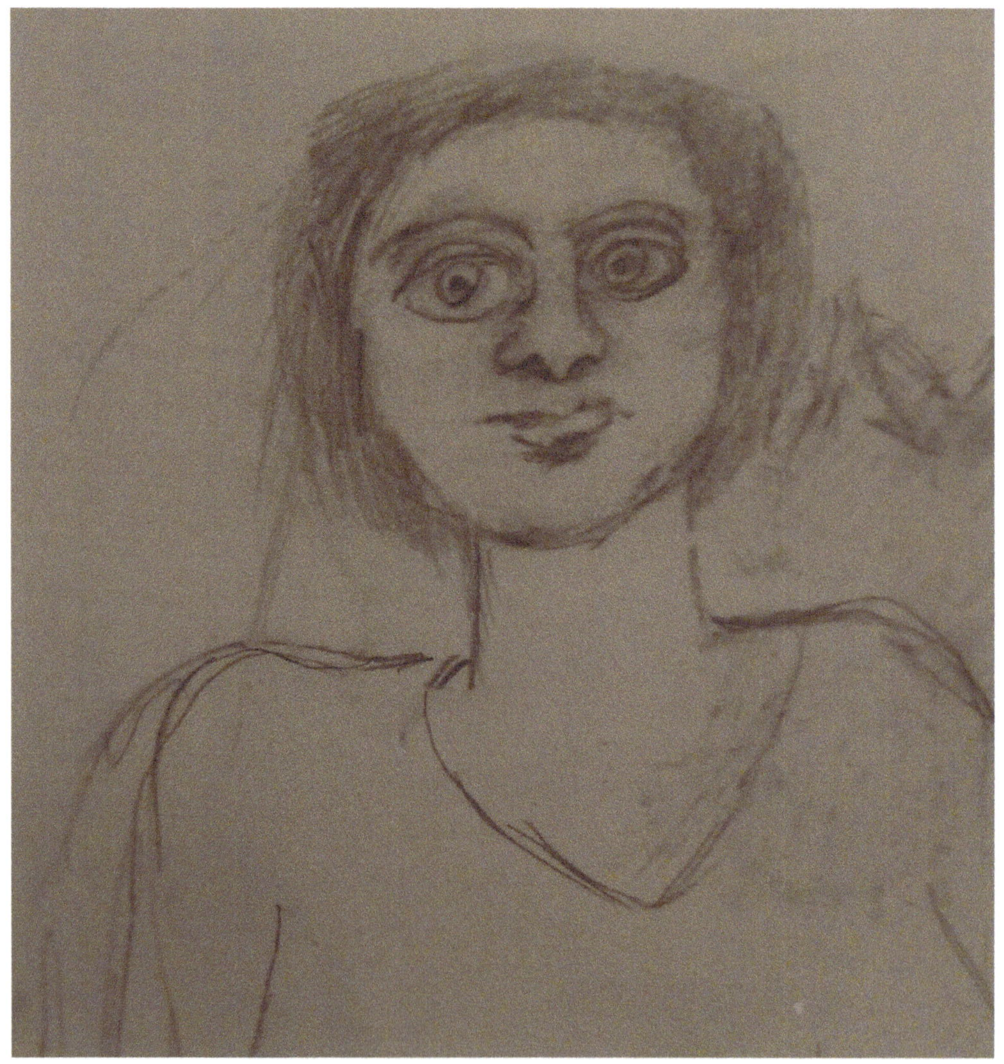

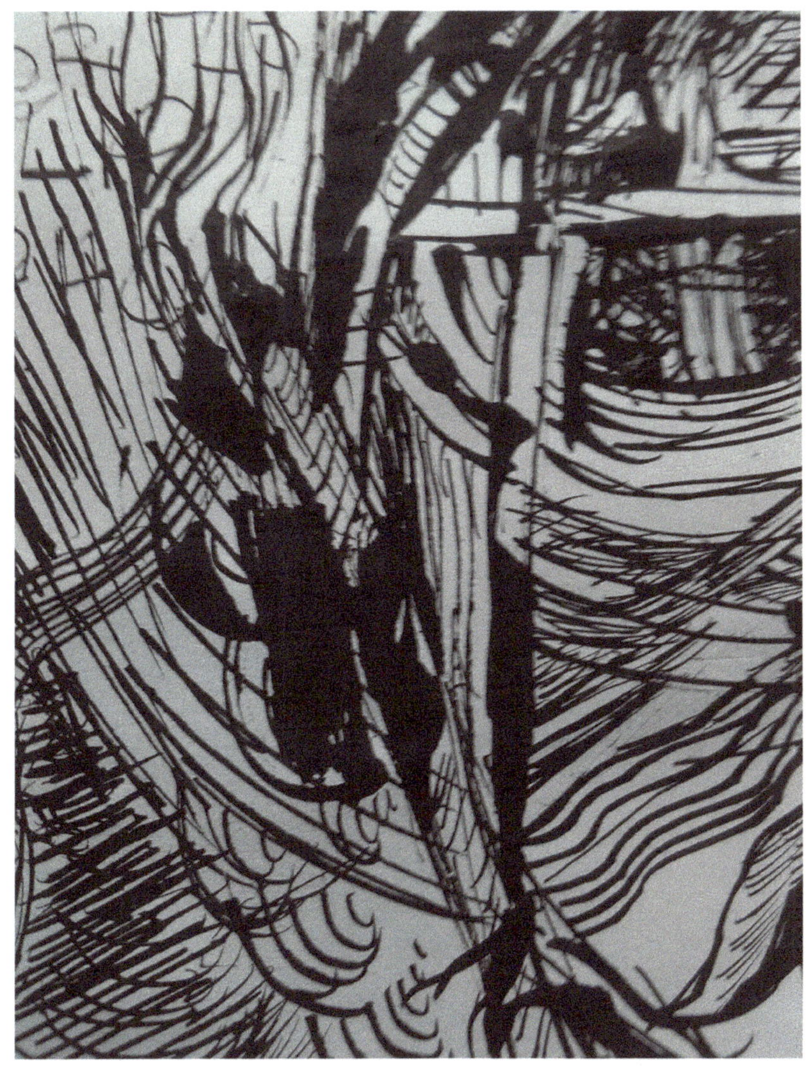

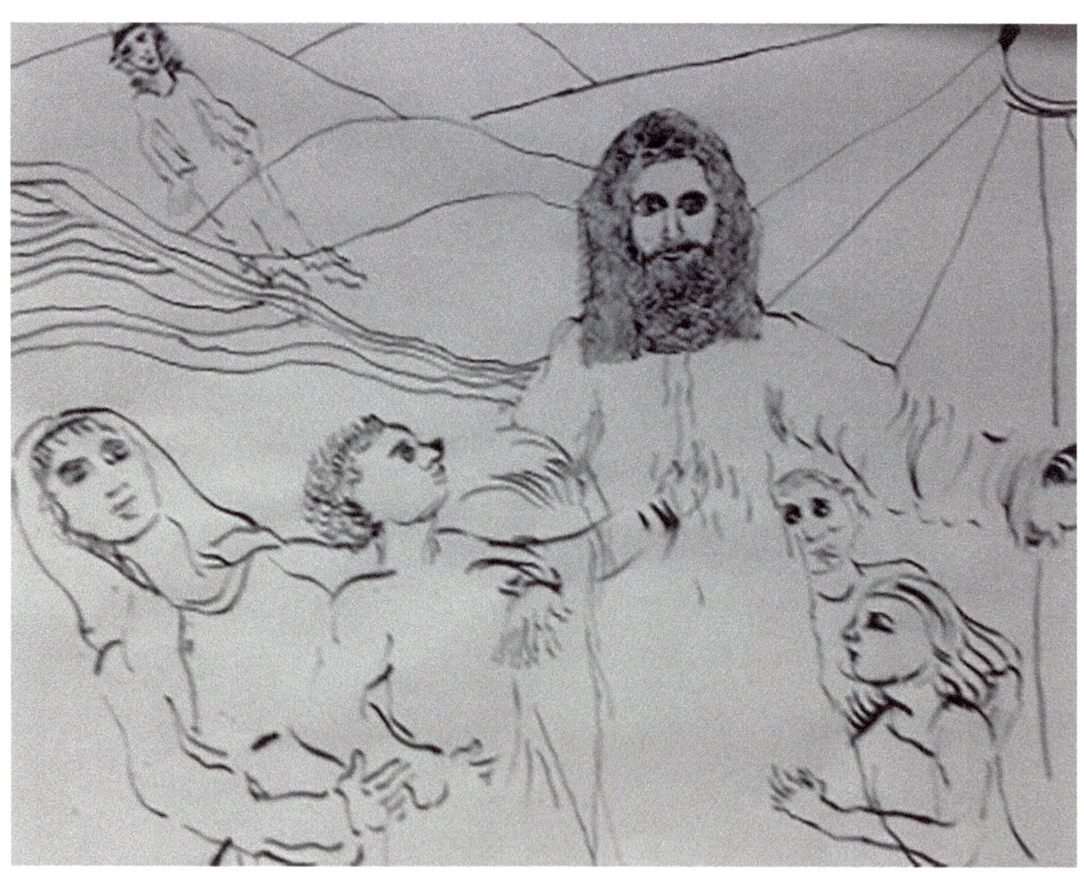

54

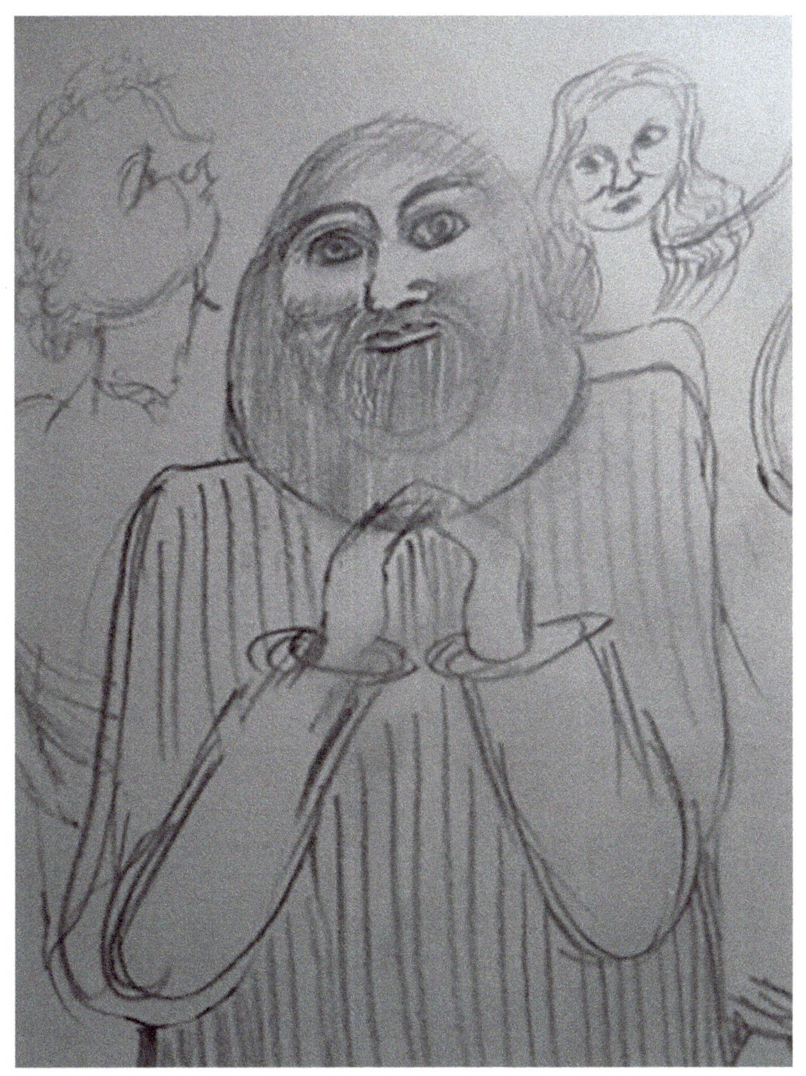

41. The Nun and the Child

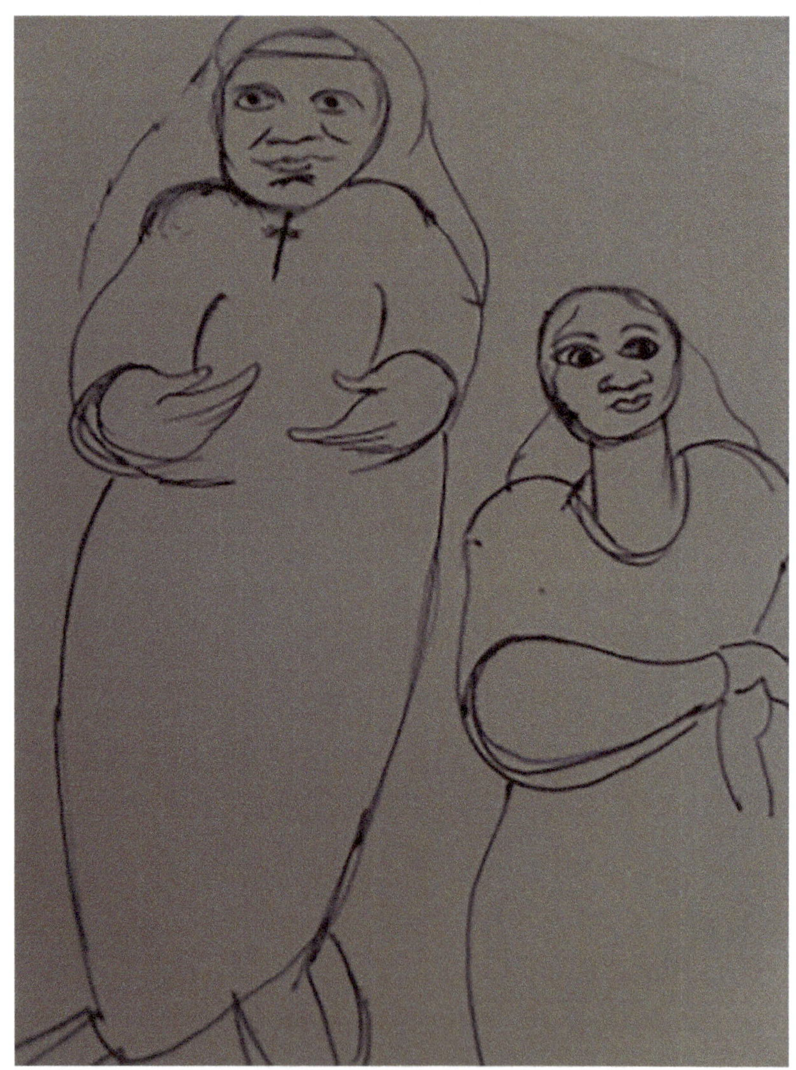

56

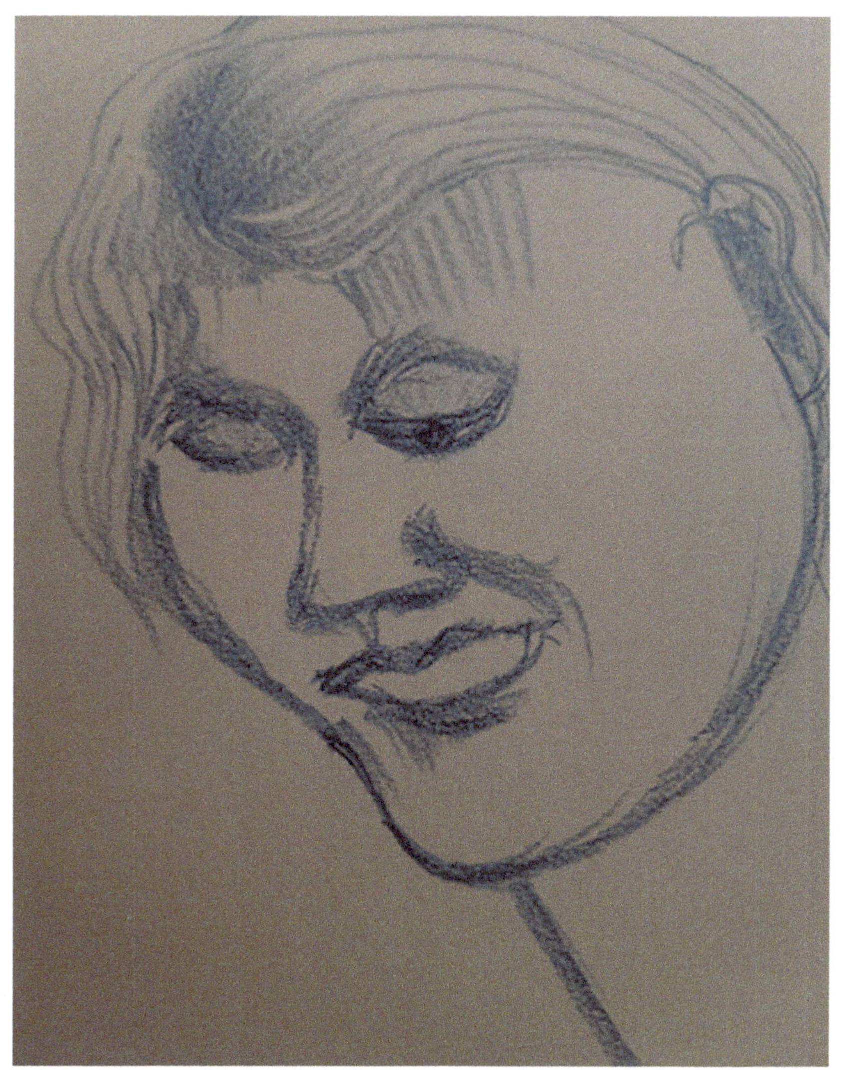

43. Mordechai Baer

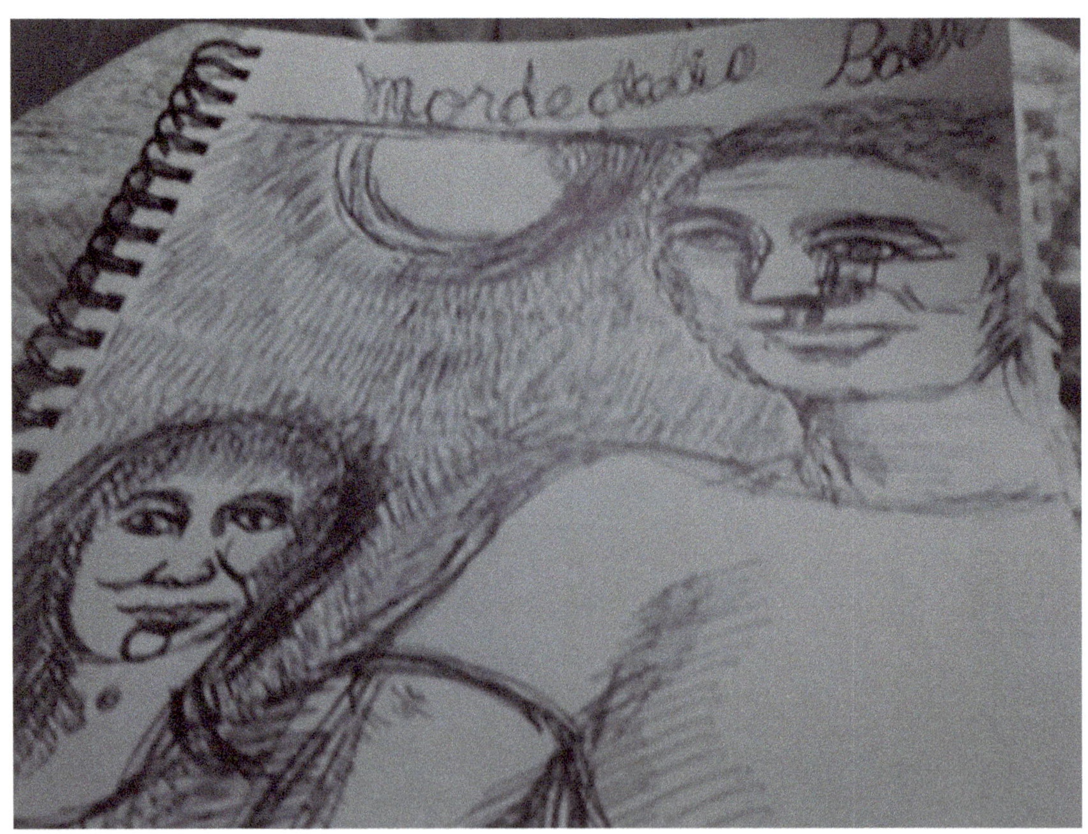

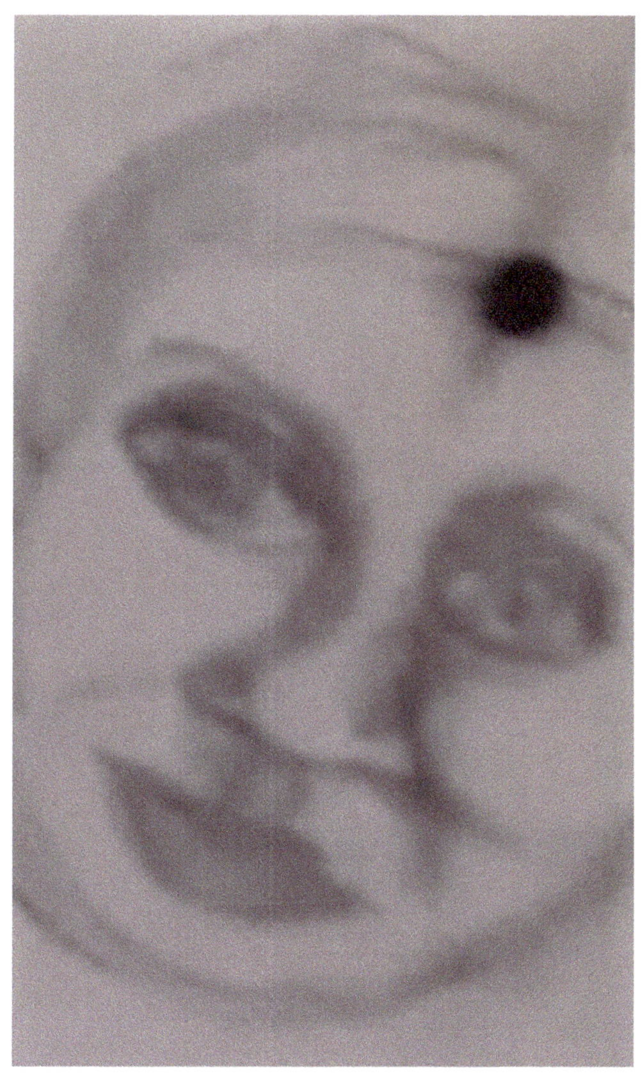

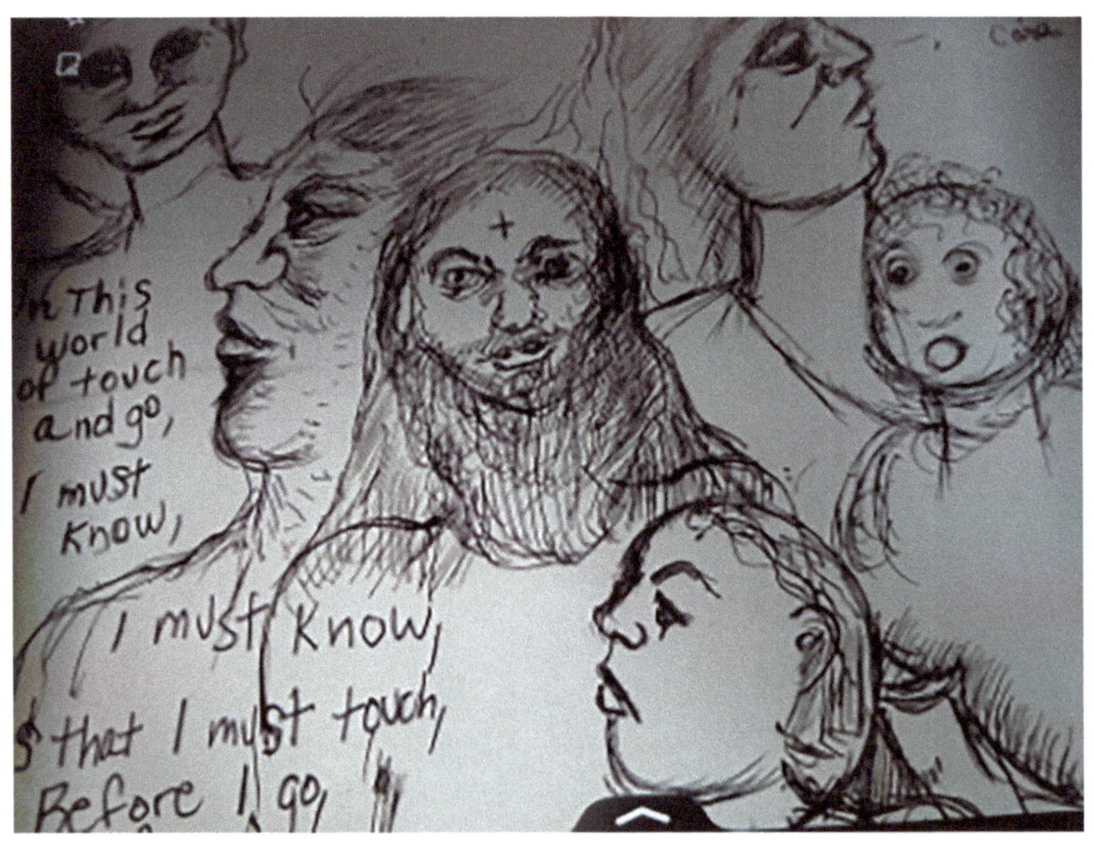

n This
world
of touch
and go,
I must
know,

I must know,

s that I must touch,
Before I go

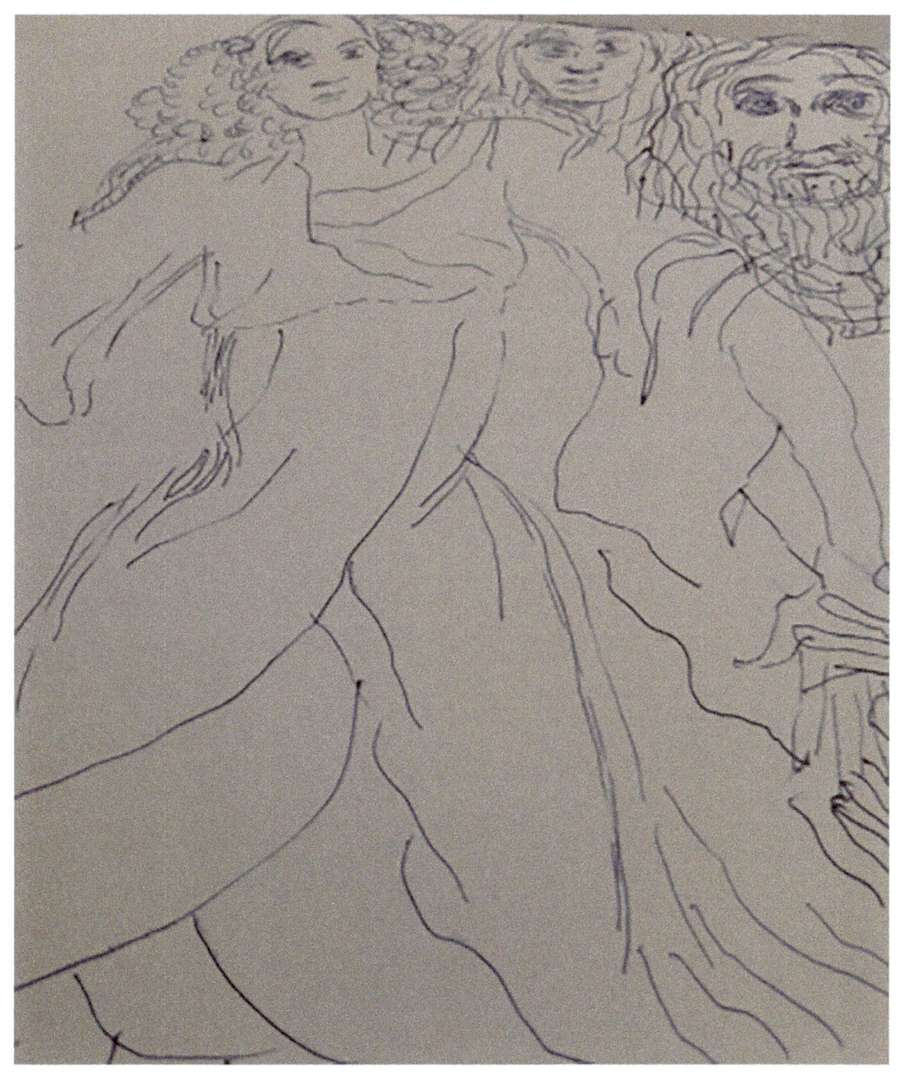

47. I and Thou

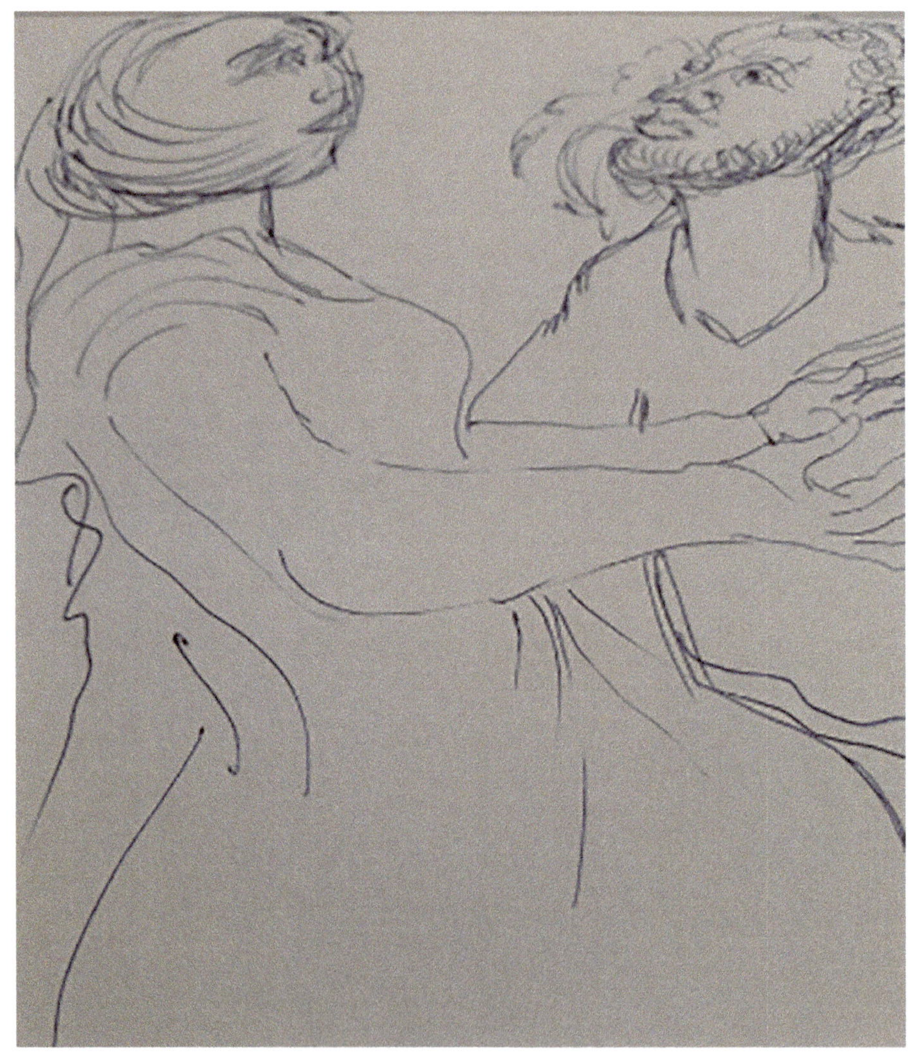

62

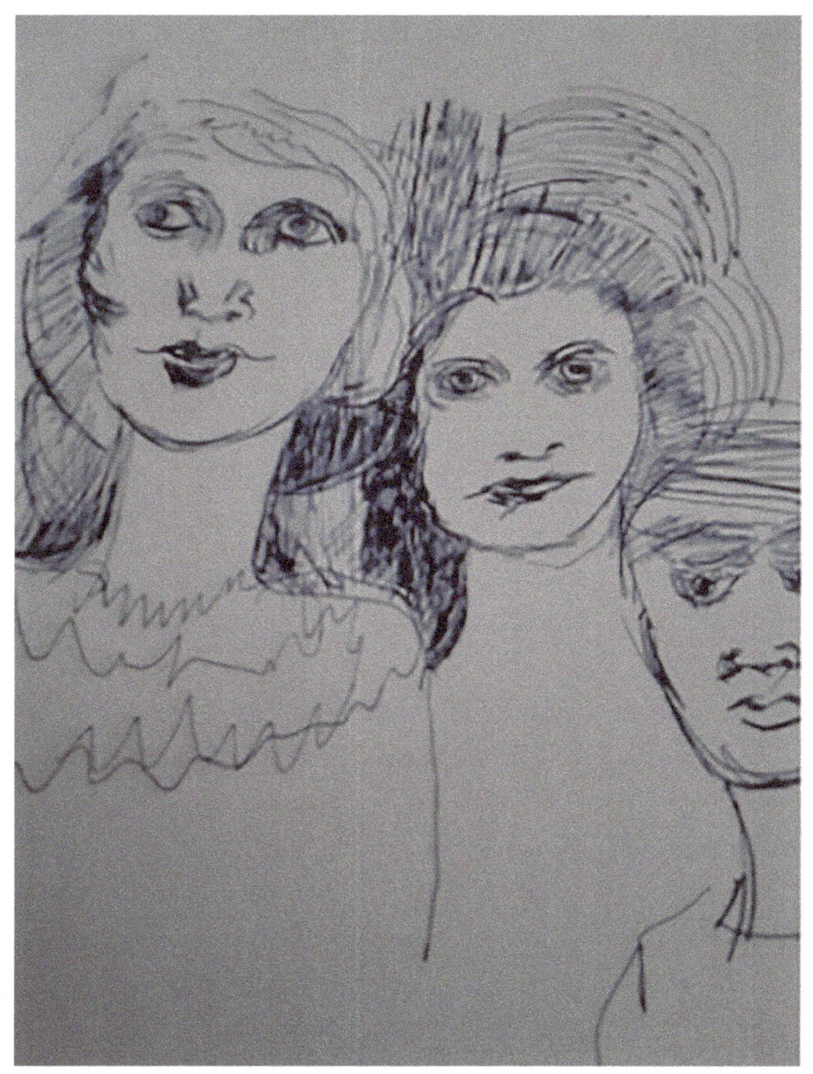

49. Three Sisters

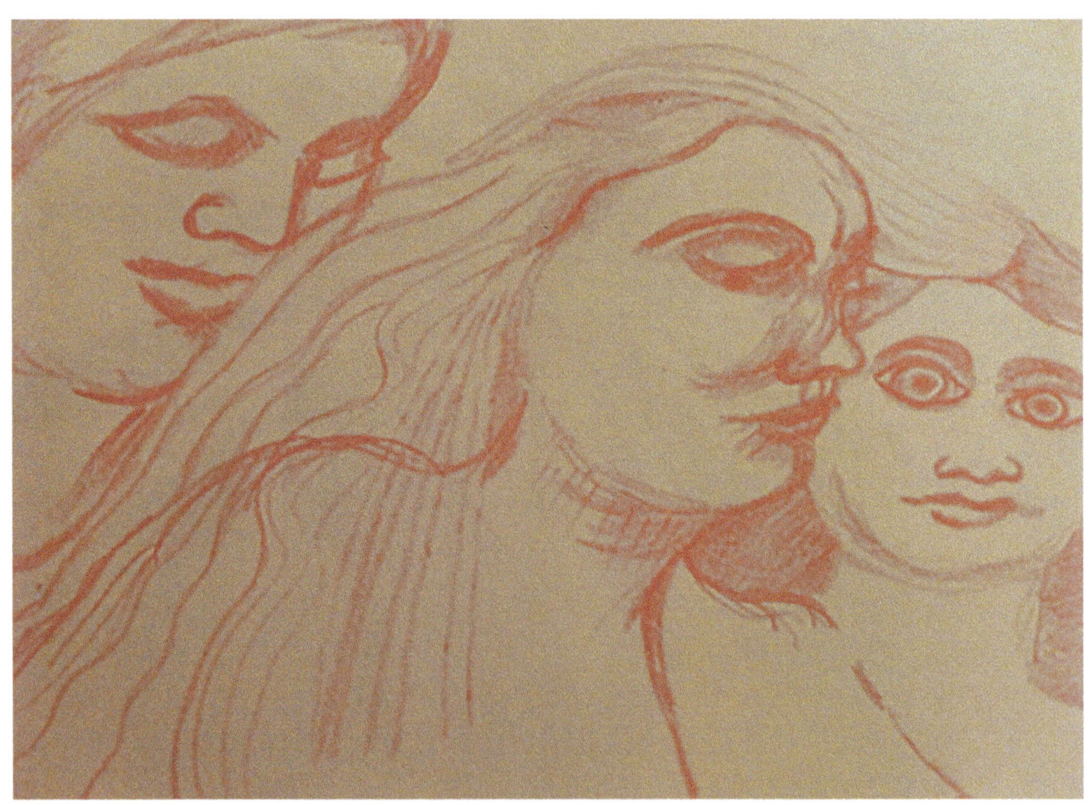

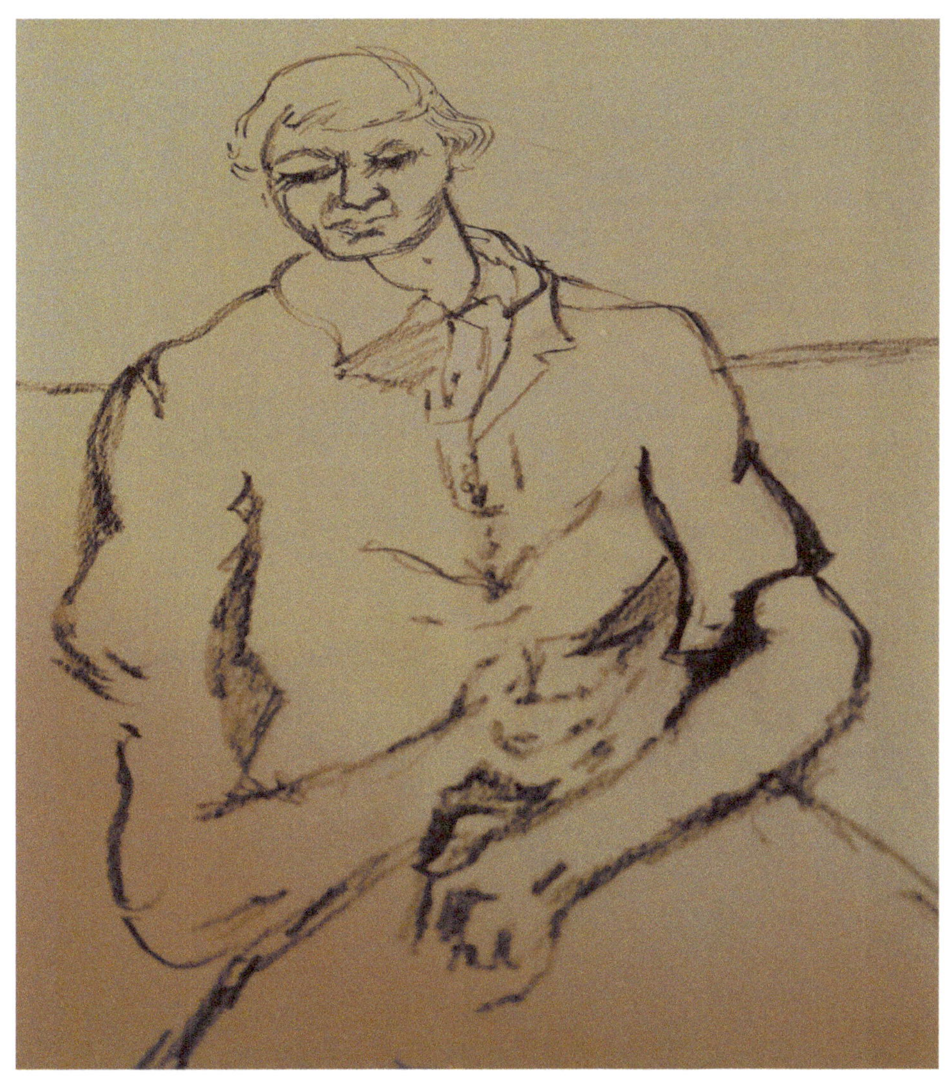

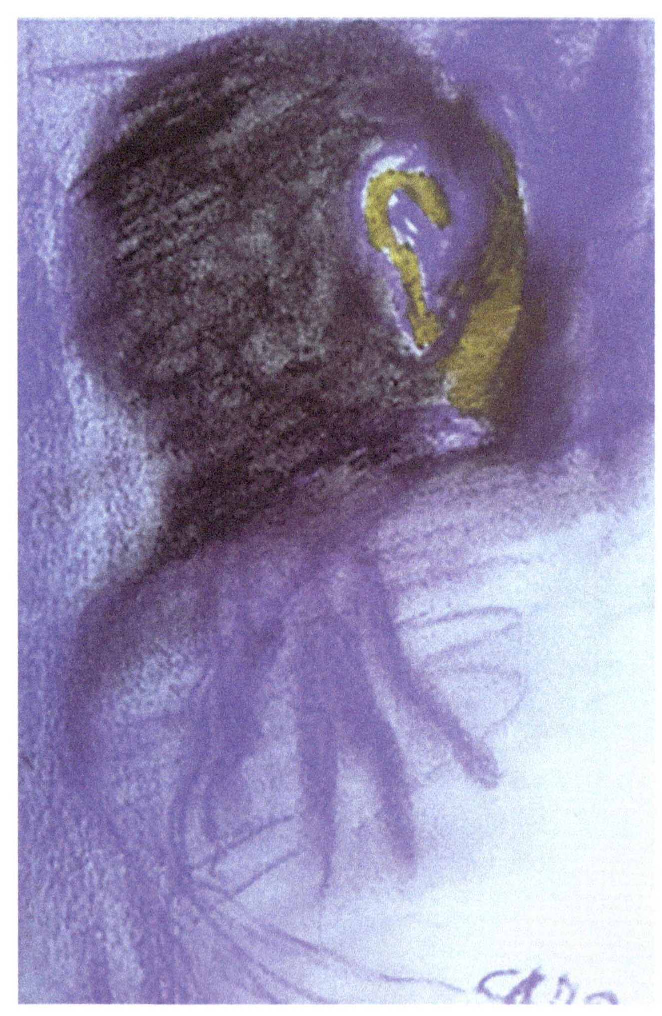

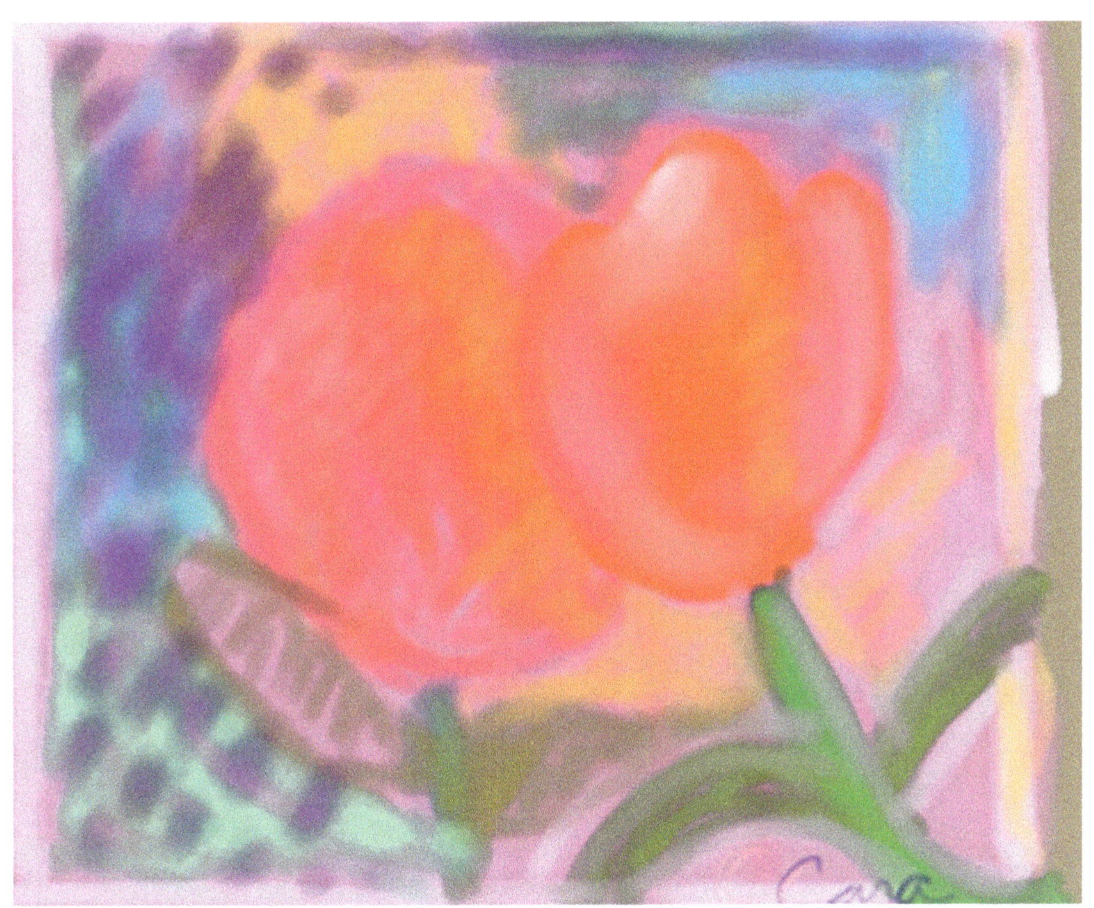

53. *Sun and the Feminine Glory*

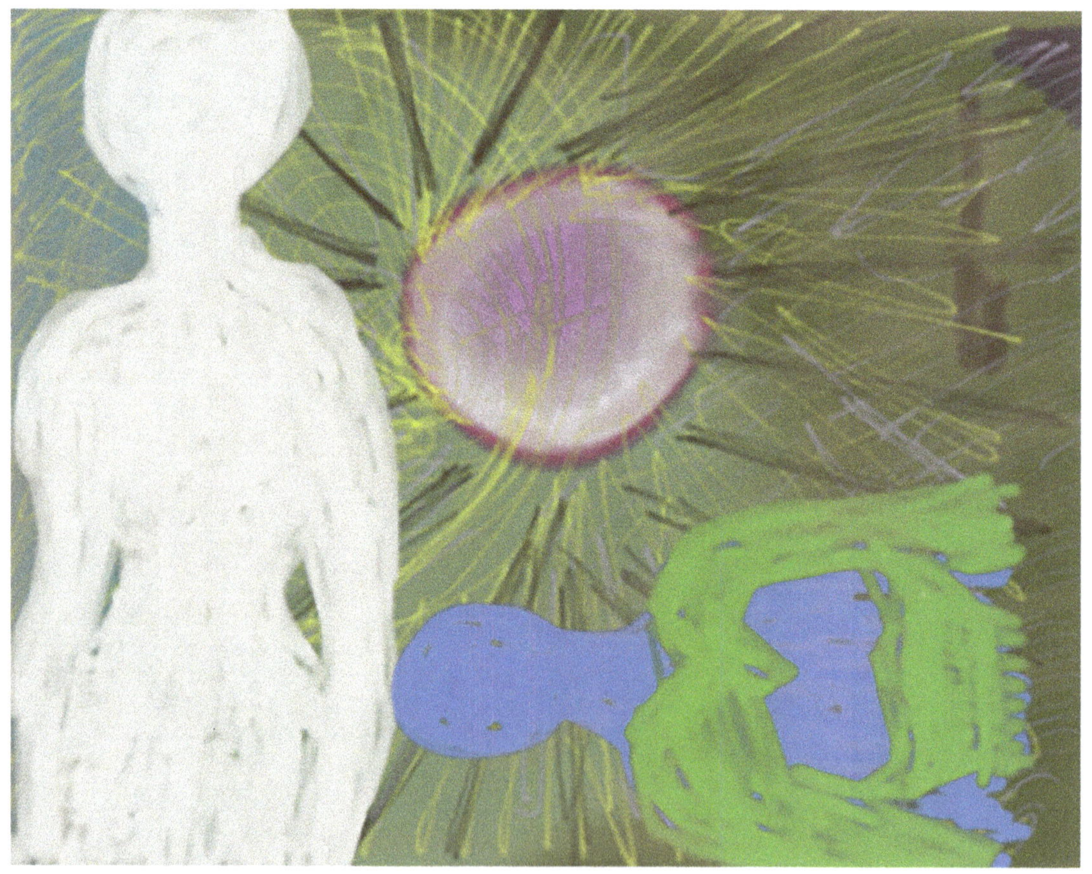

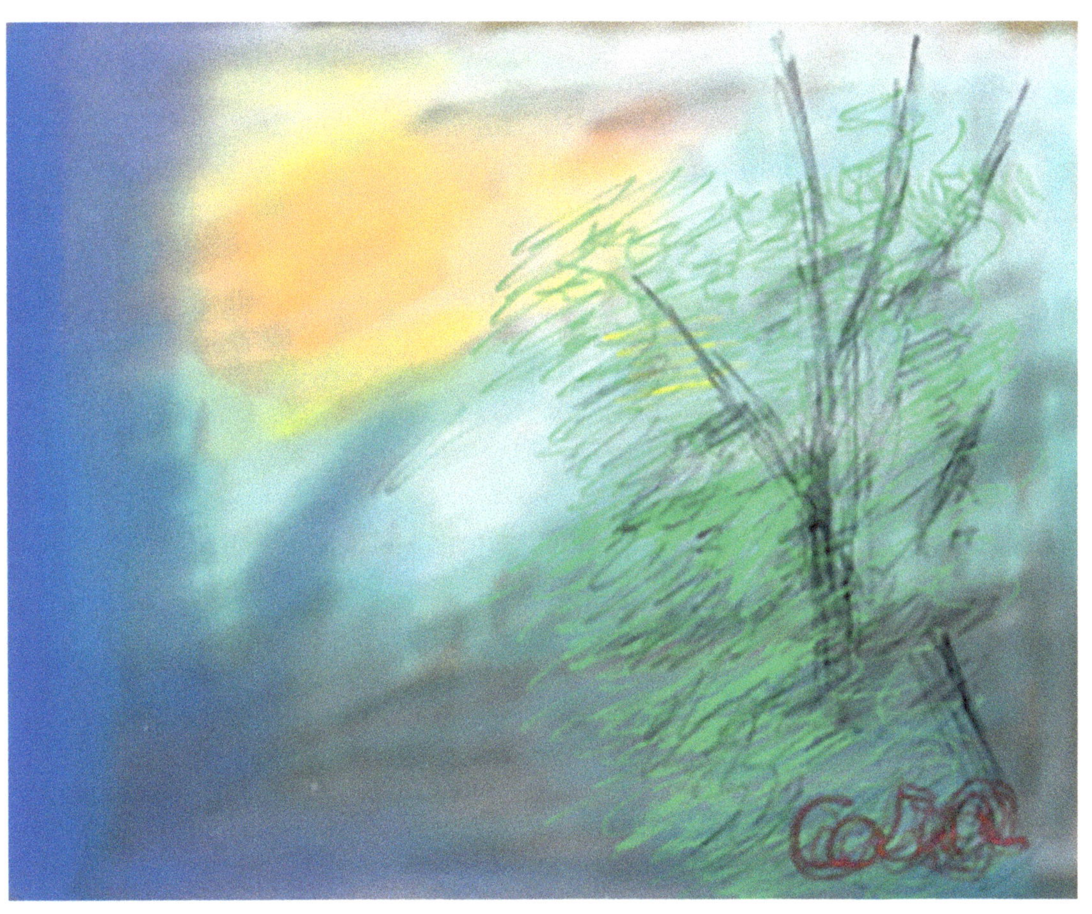

55. Flower in Atmosphere

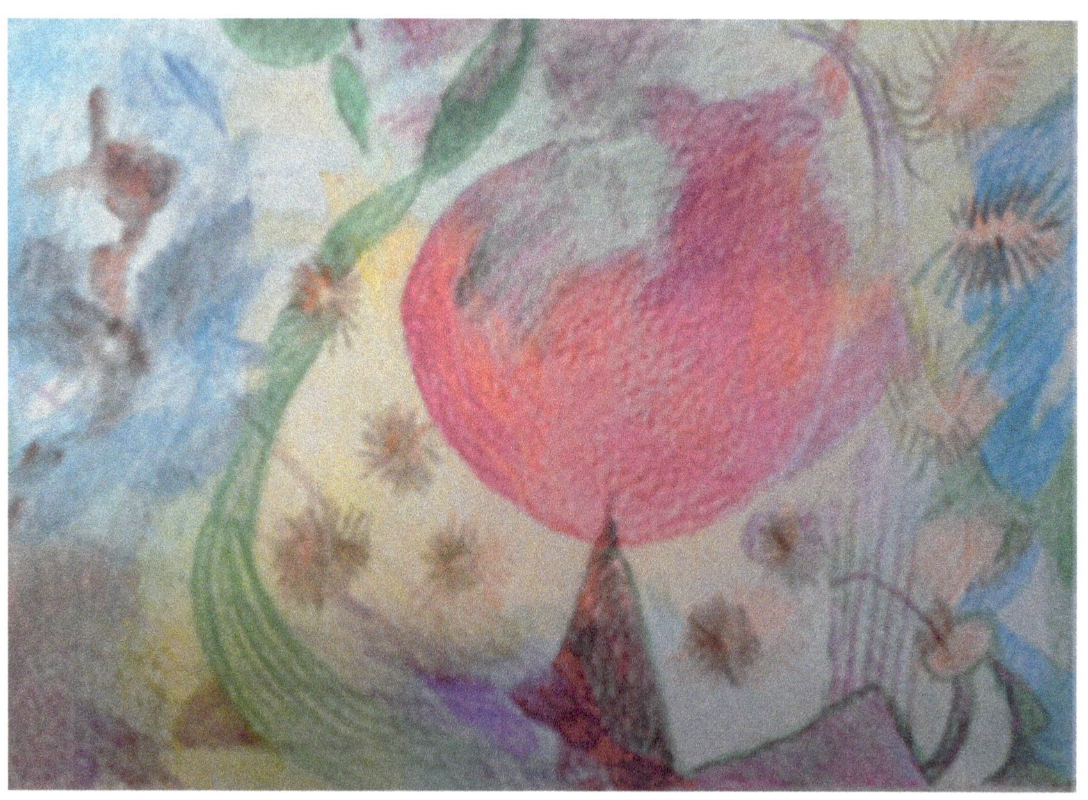

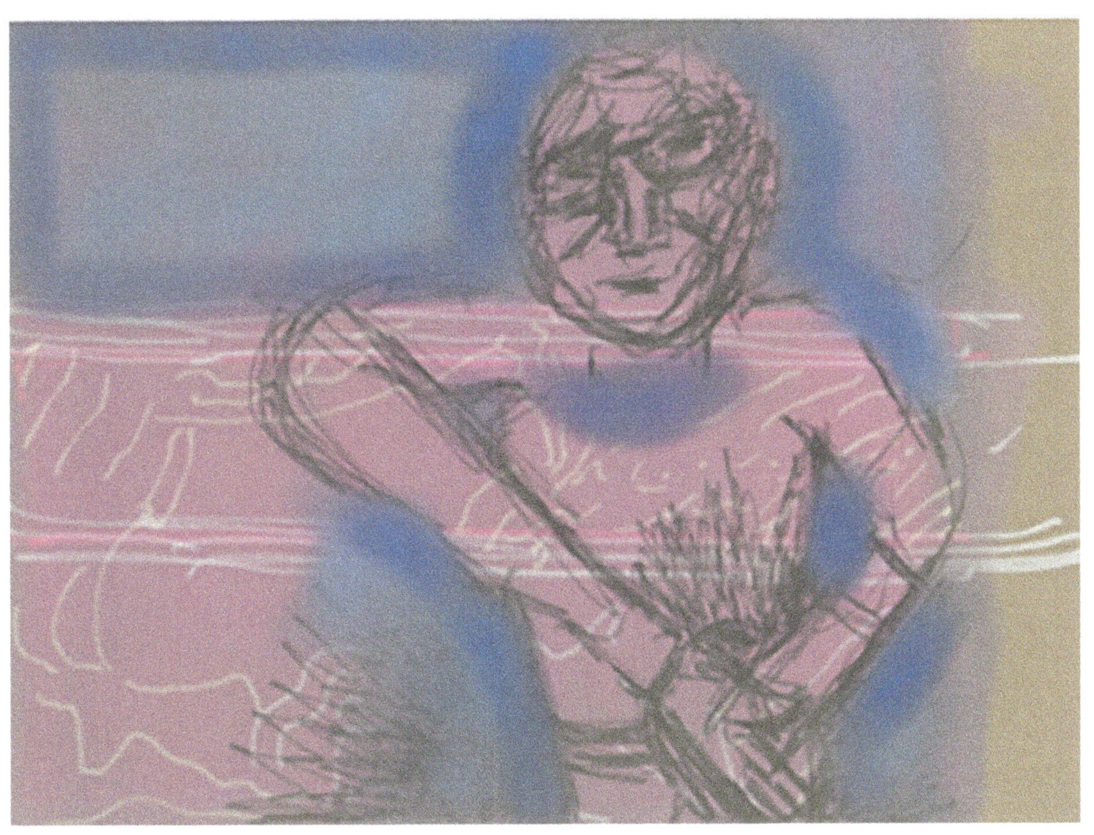

57. People, Hearts, Stars

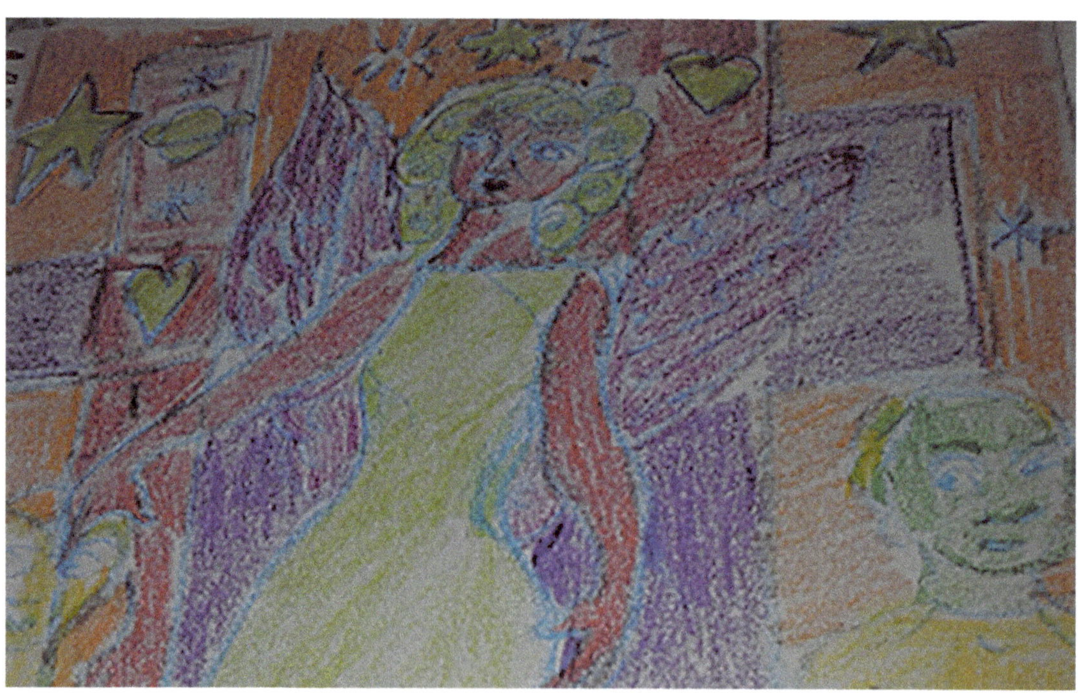

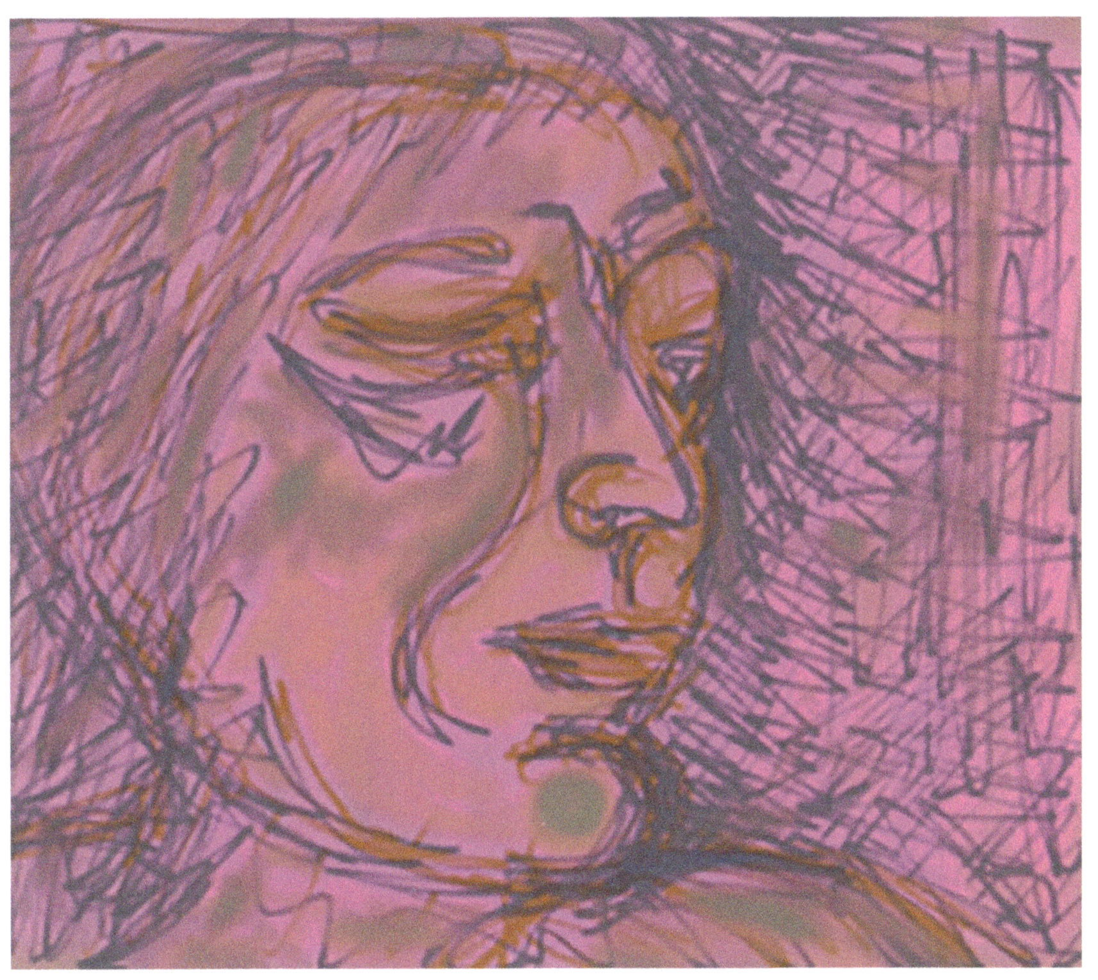

58. Portrait of Joseph

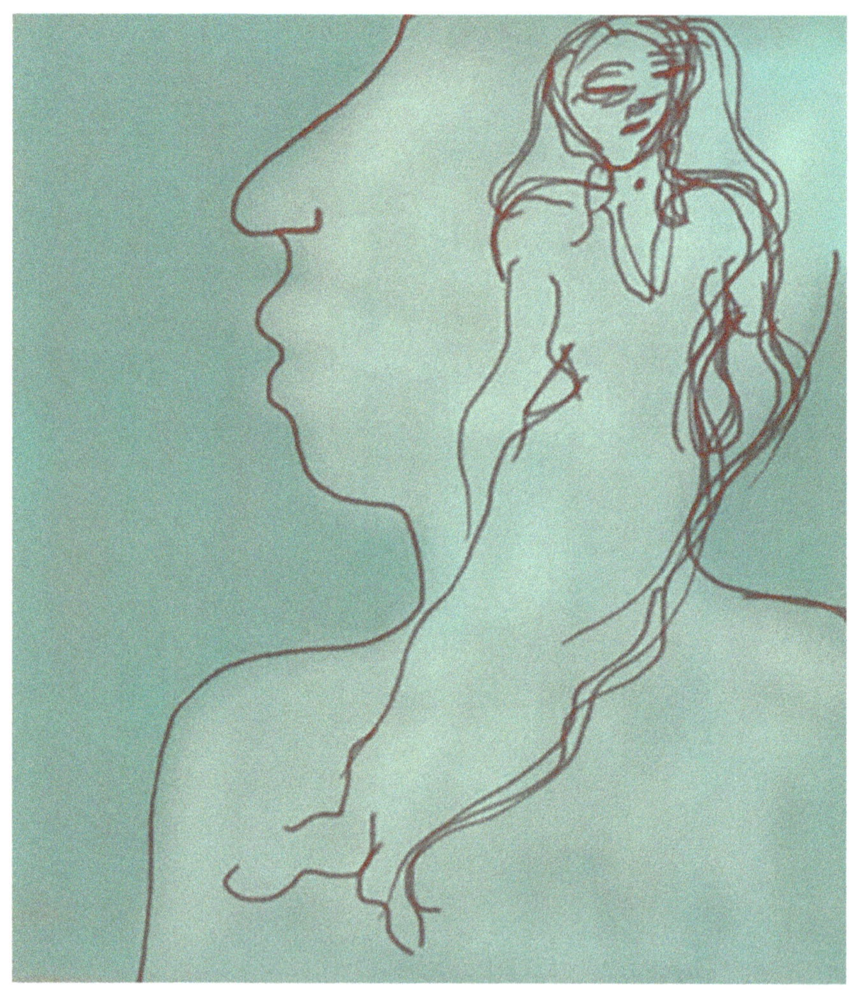

60. Portrait of My Father

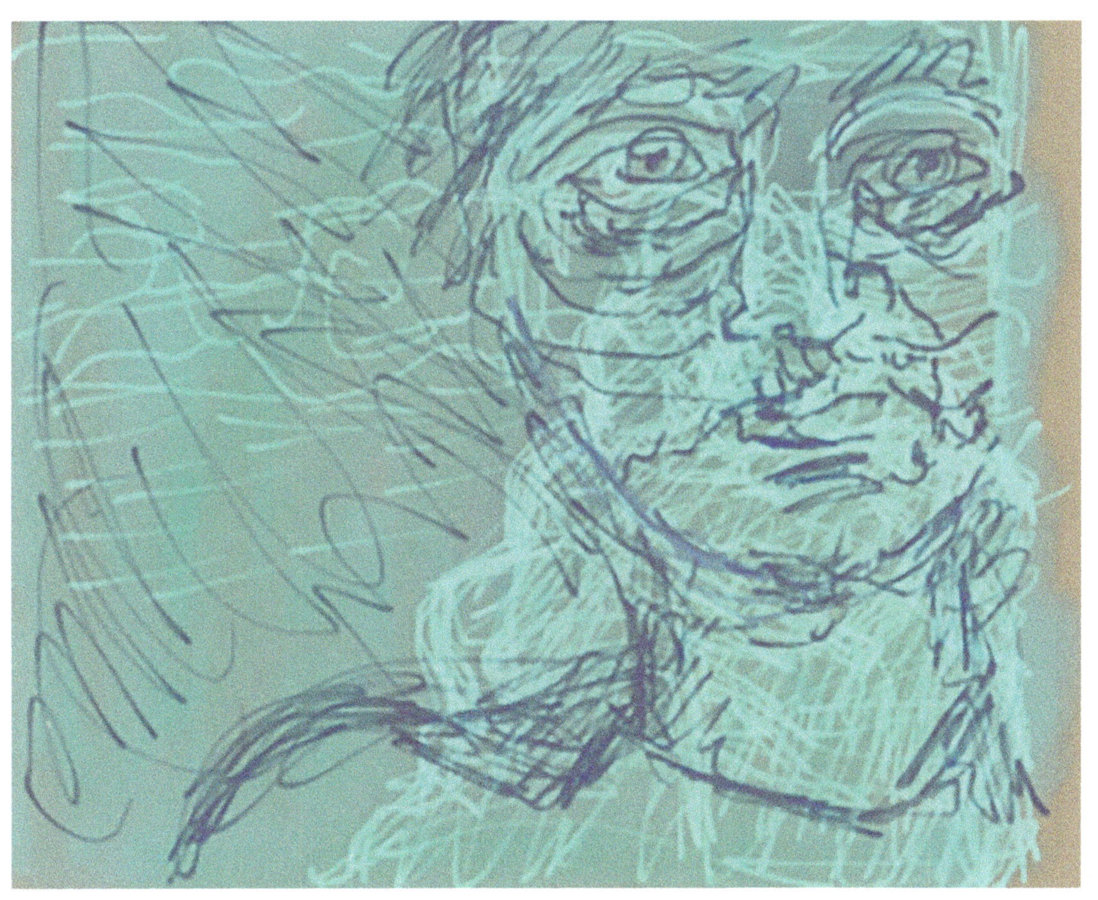

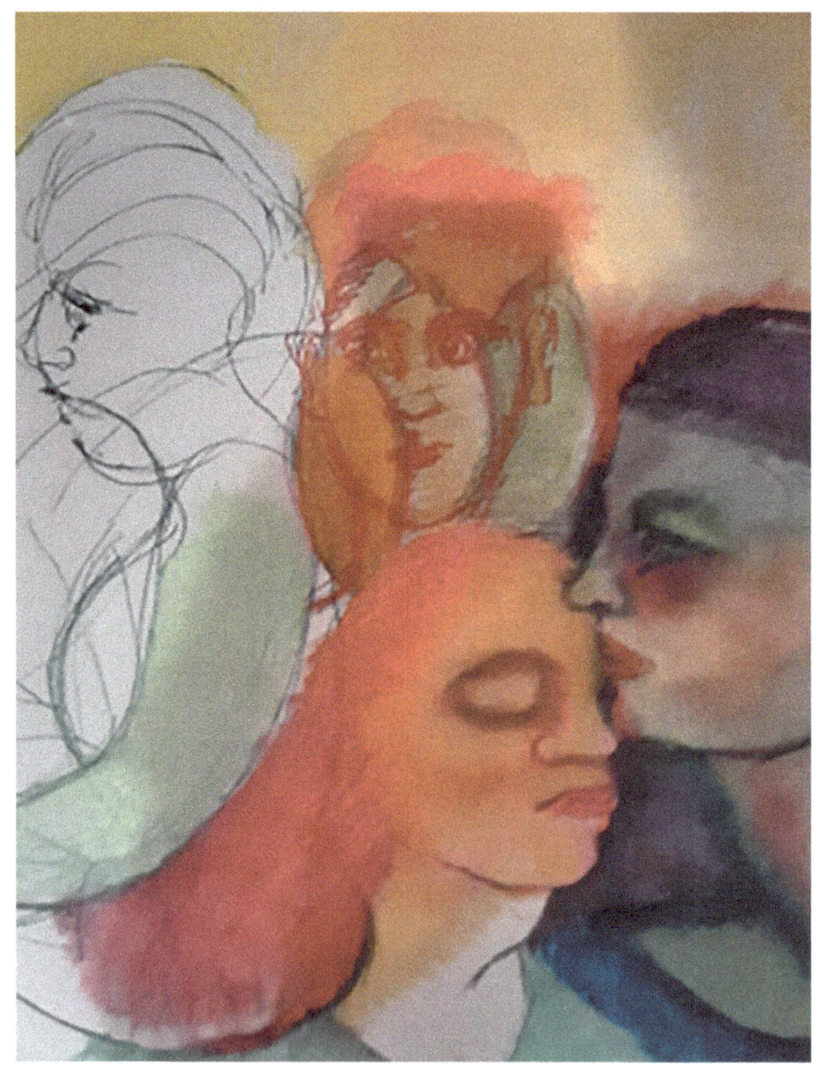

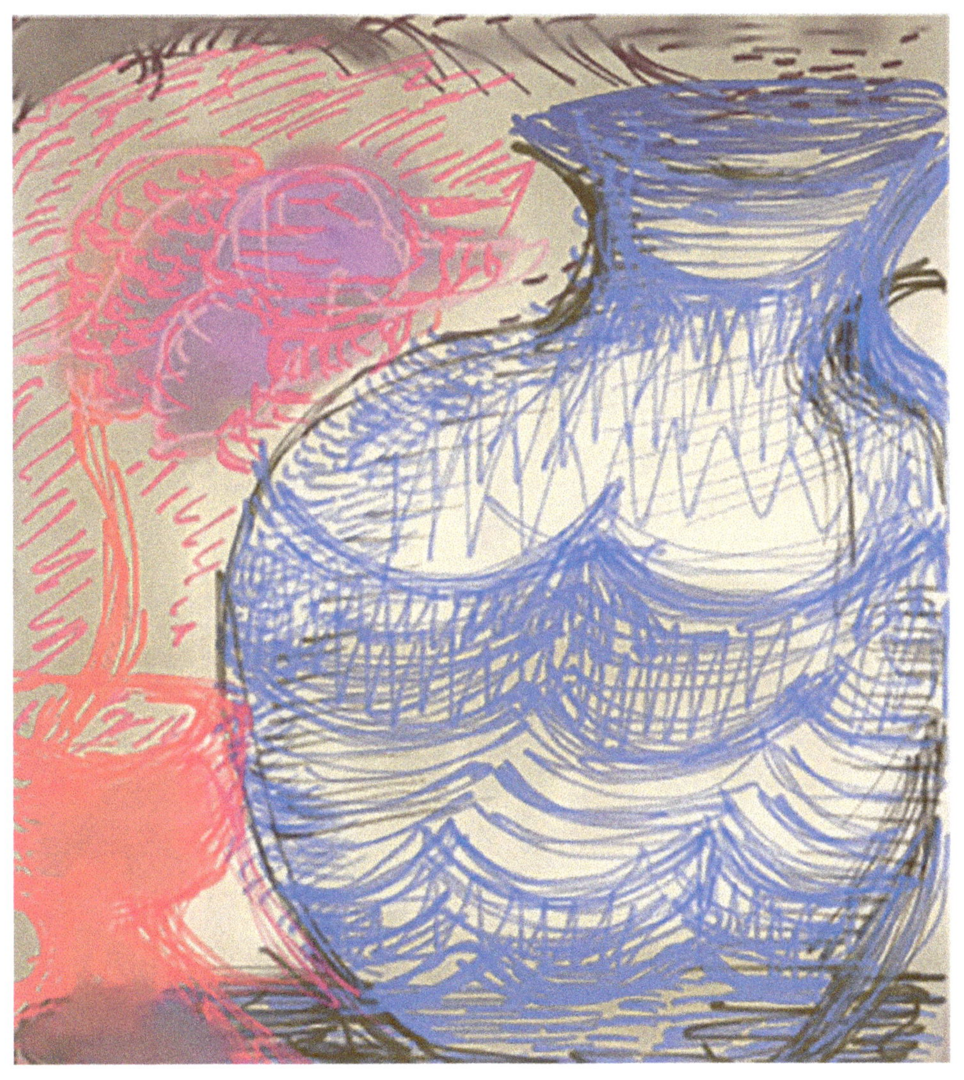

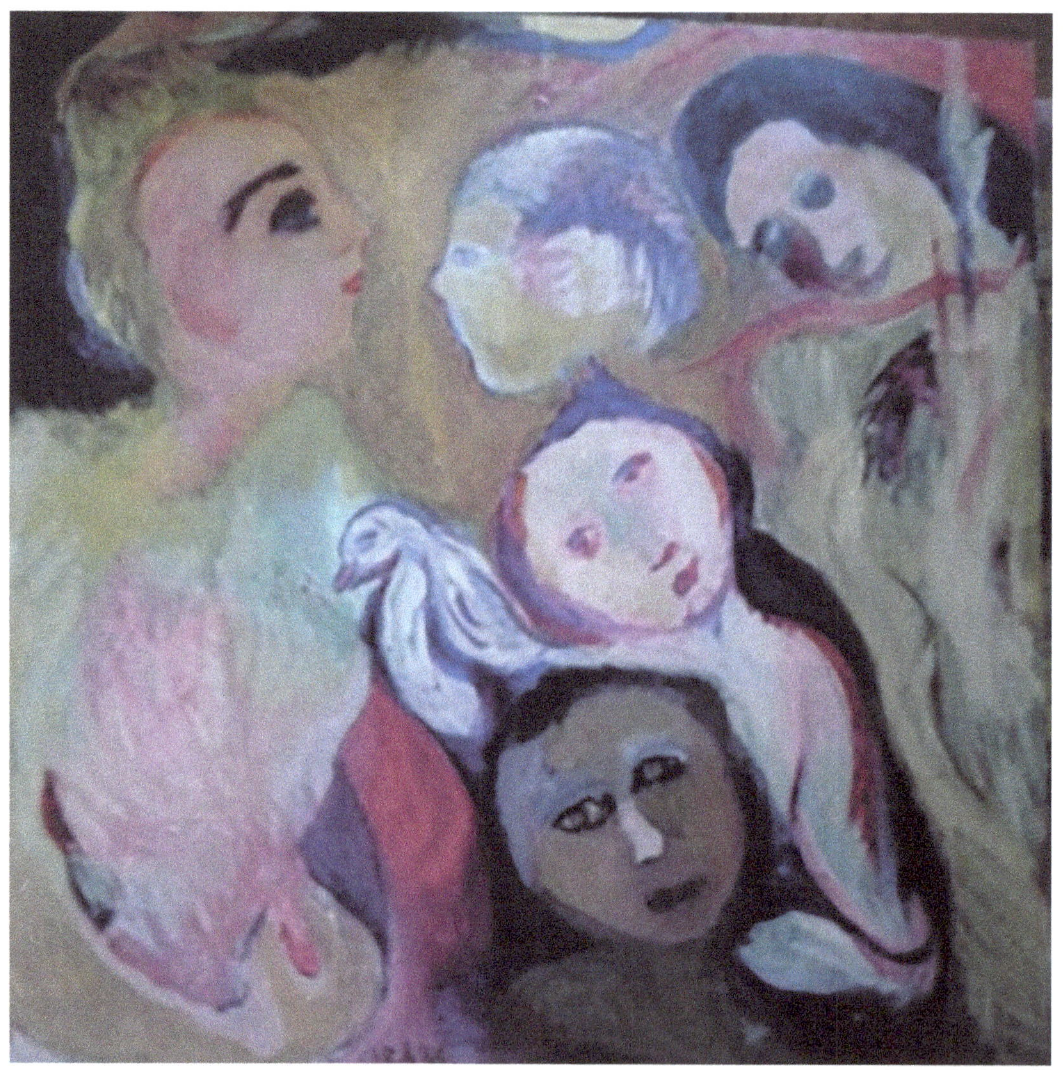

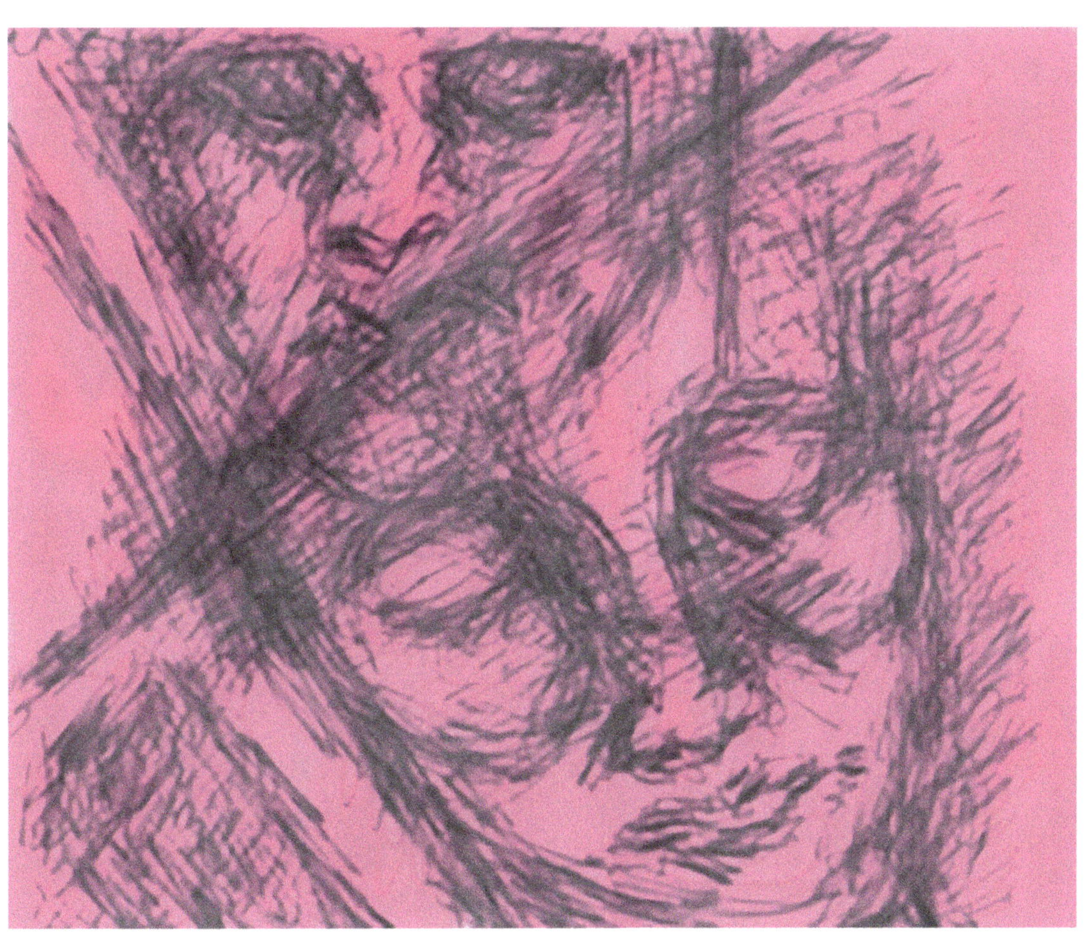

65. Jesus Stars

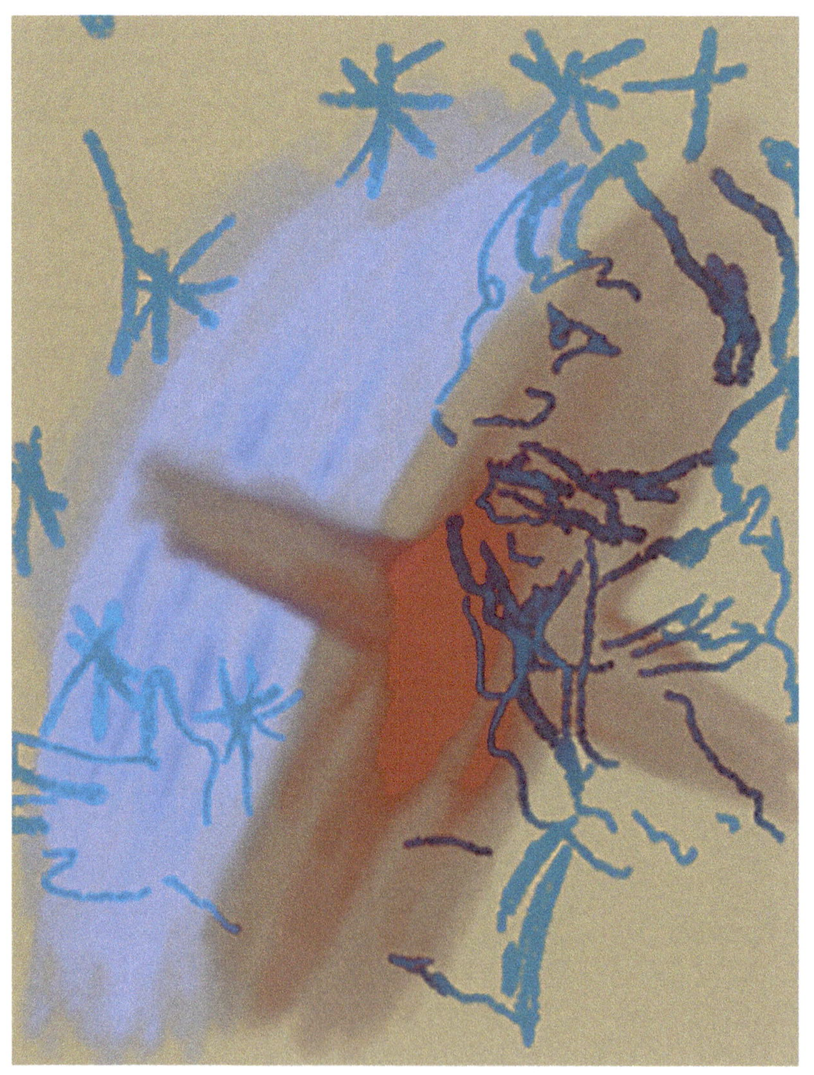

80

66. A Strong Woman

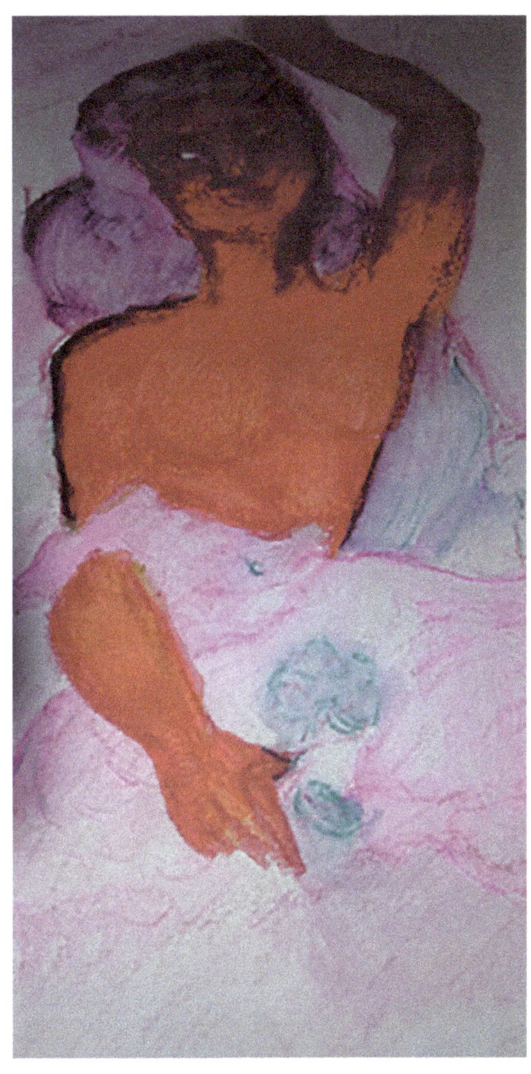

67. Moorman

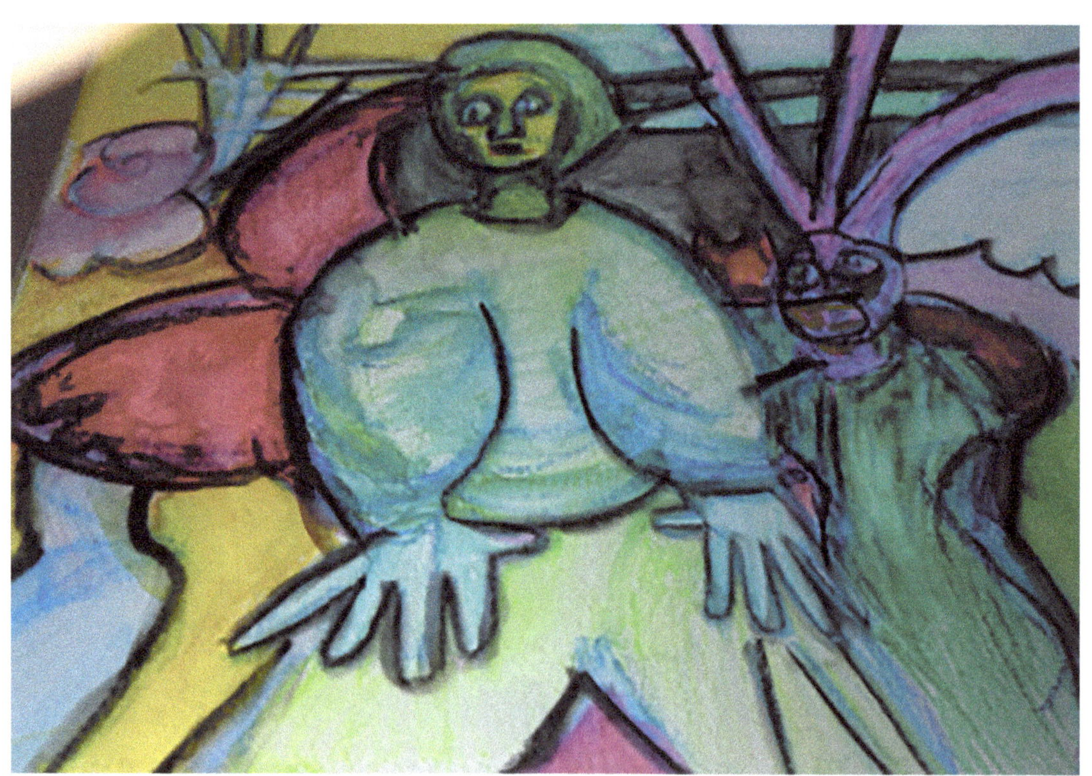

68. Father and Son

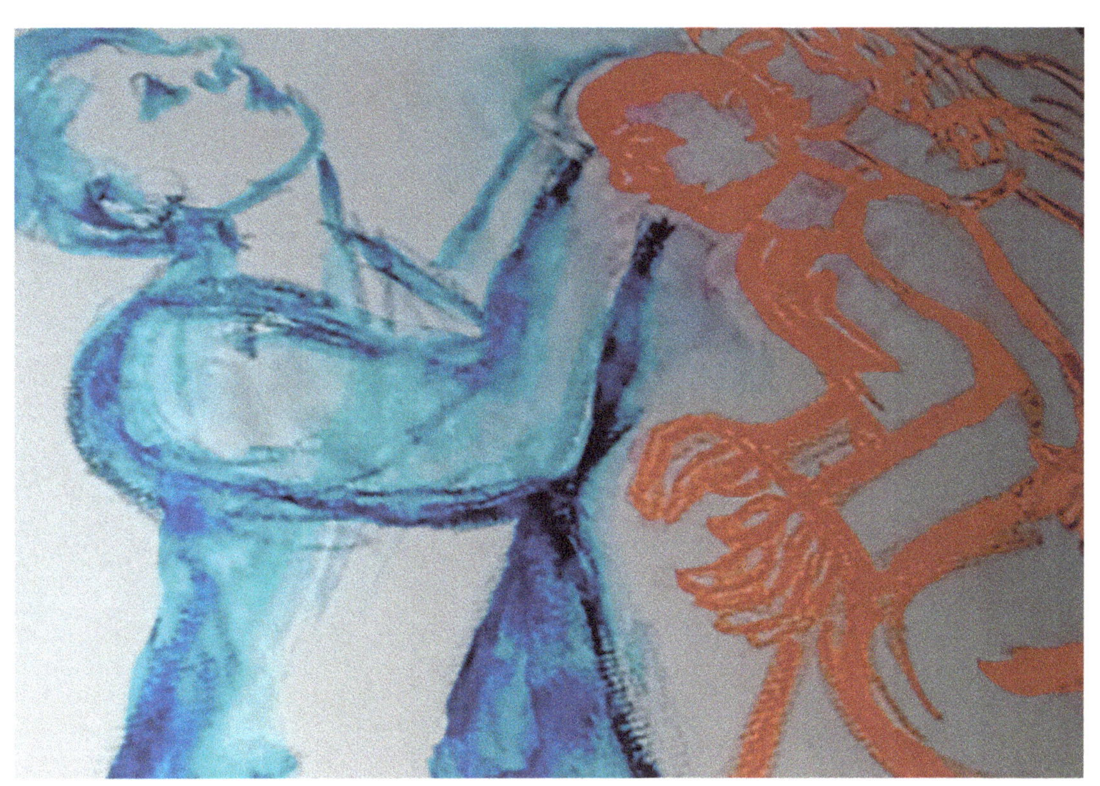

69. Two in Love

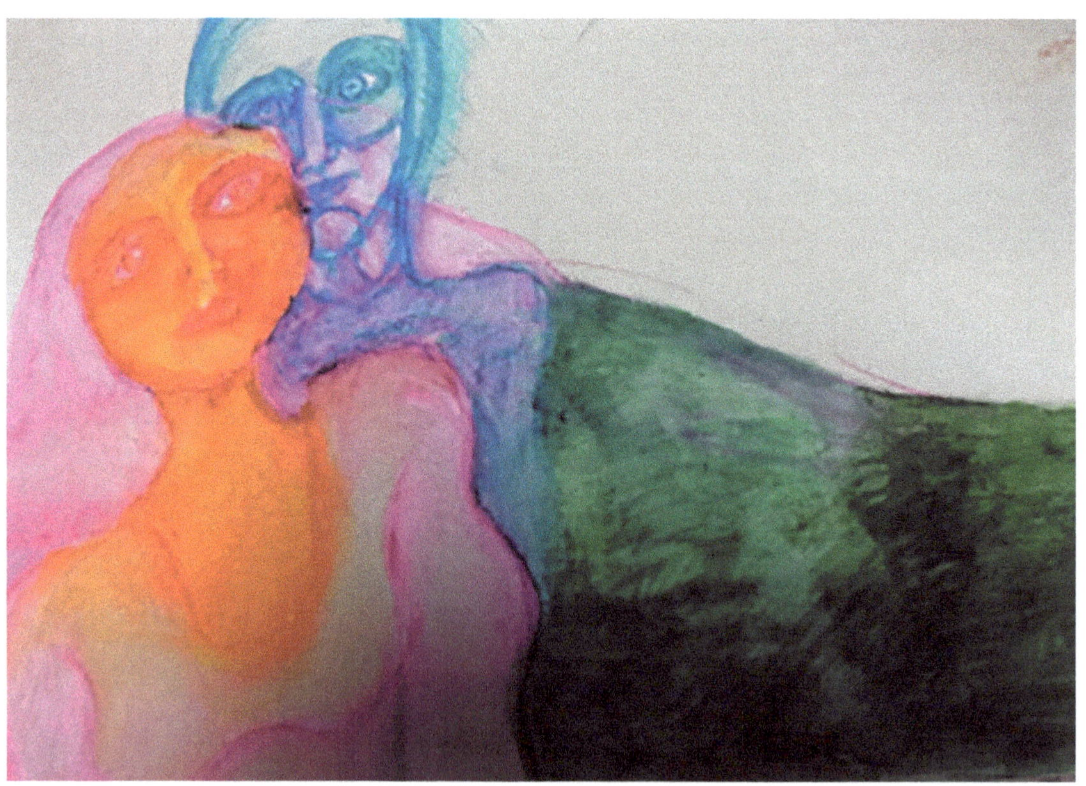

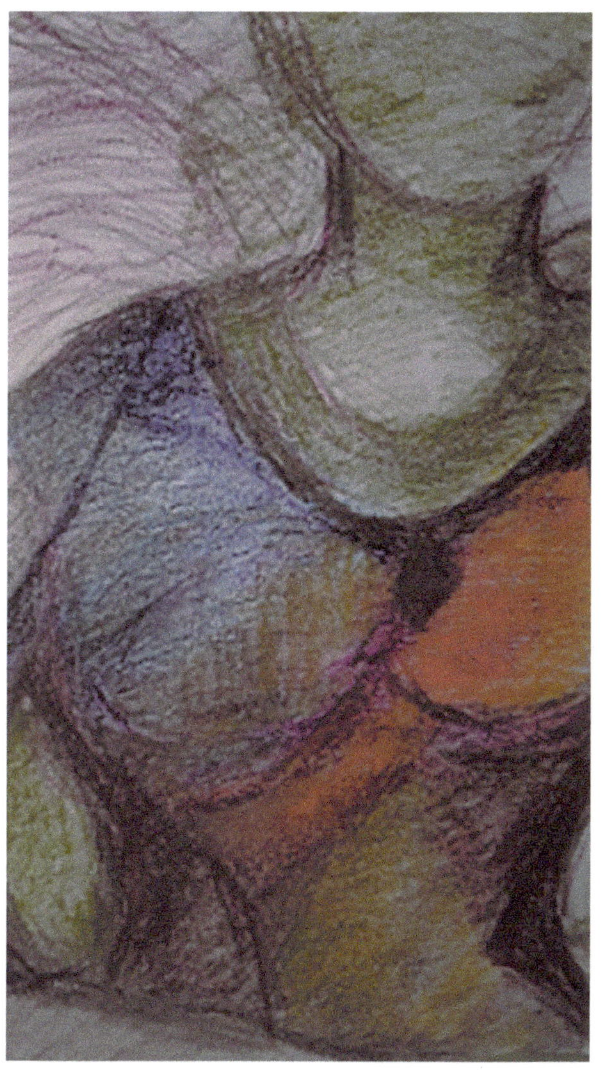

71. Aging Along

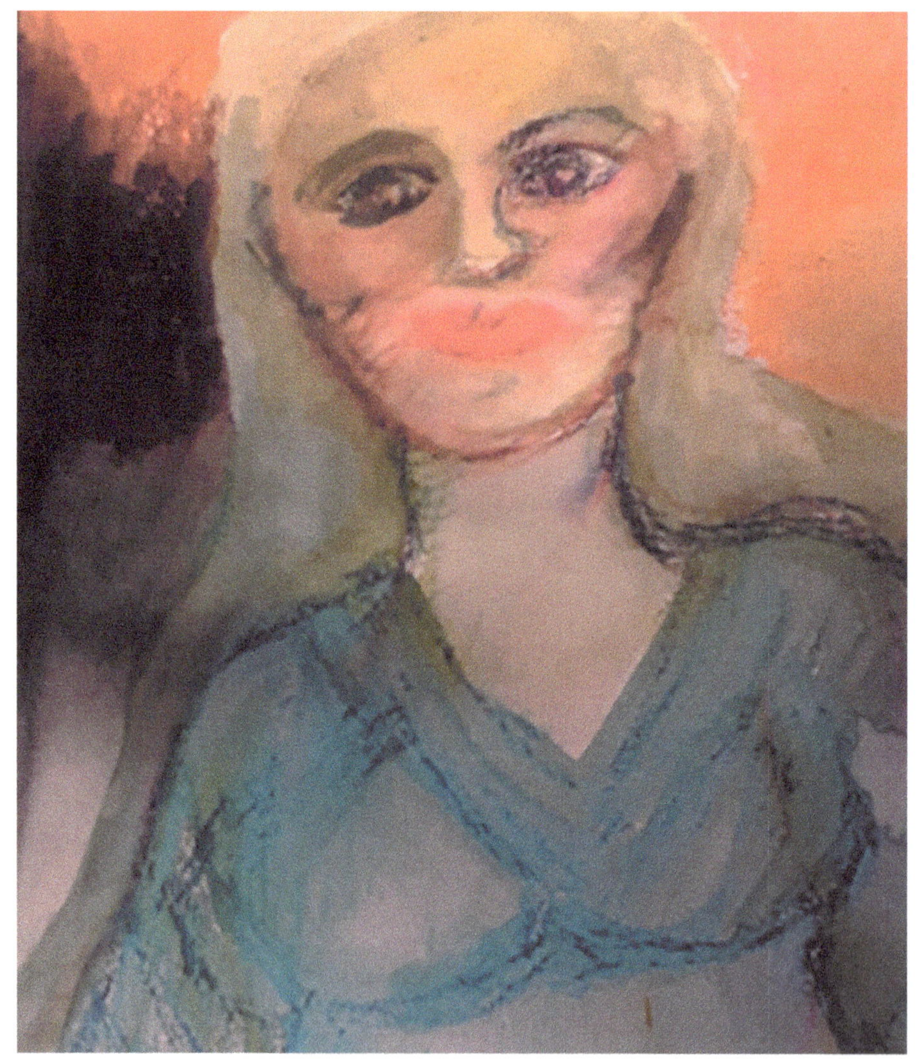

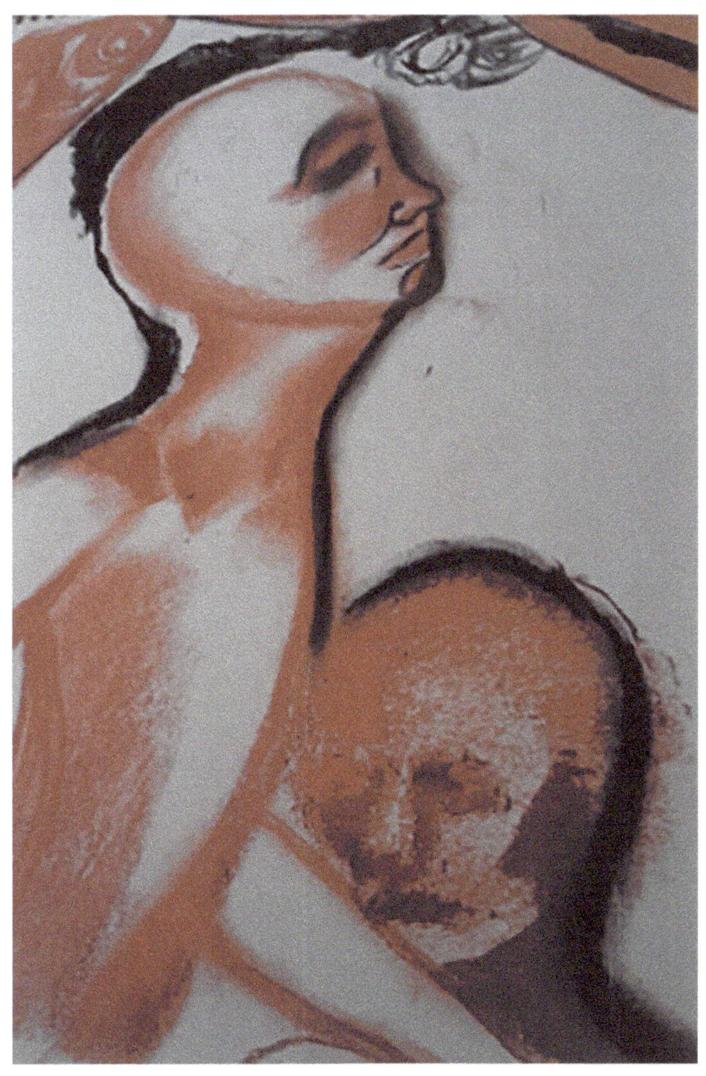

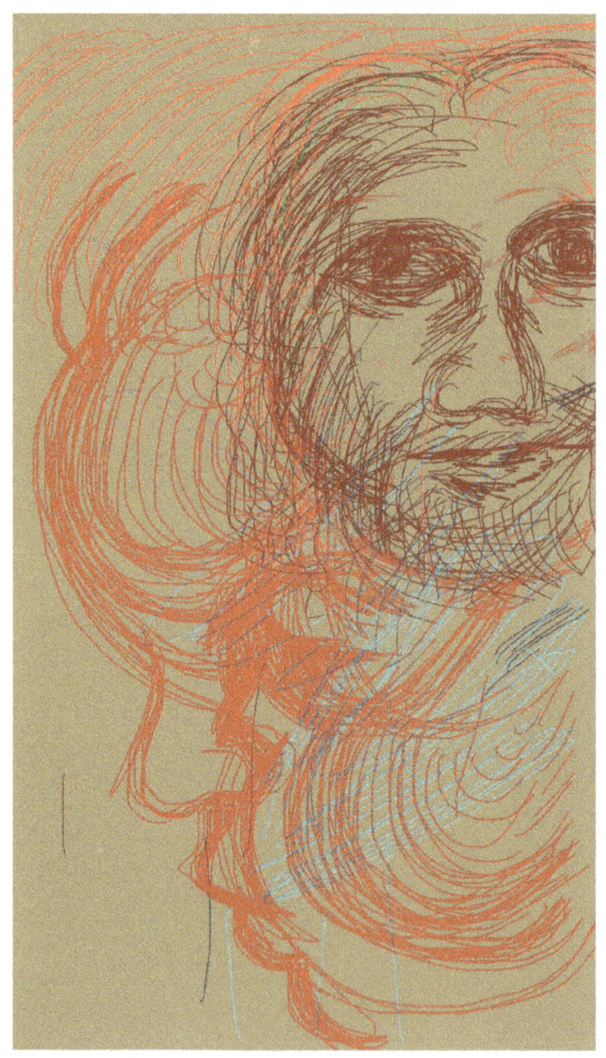

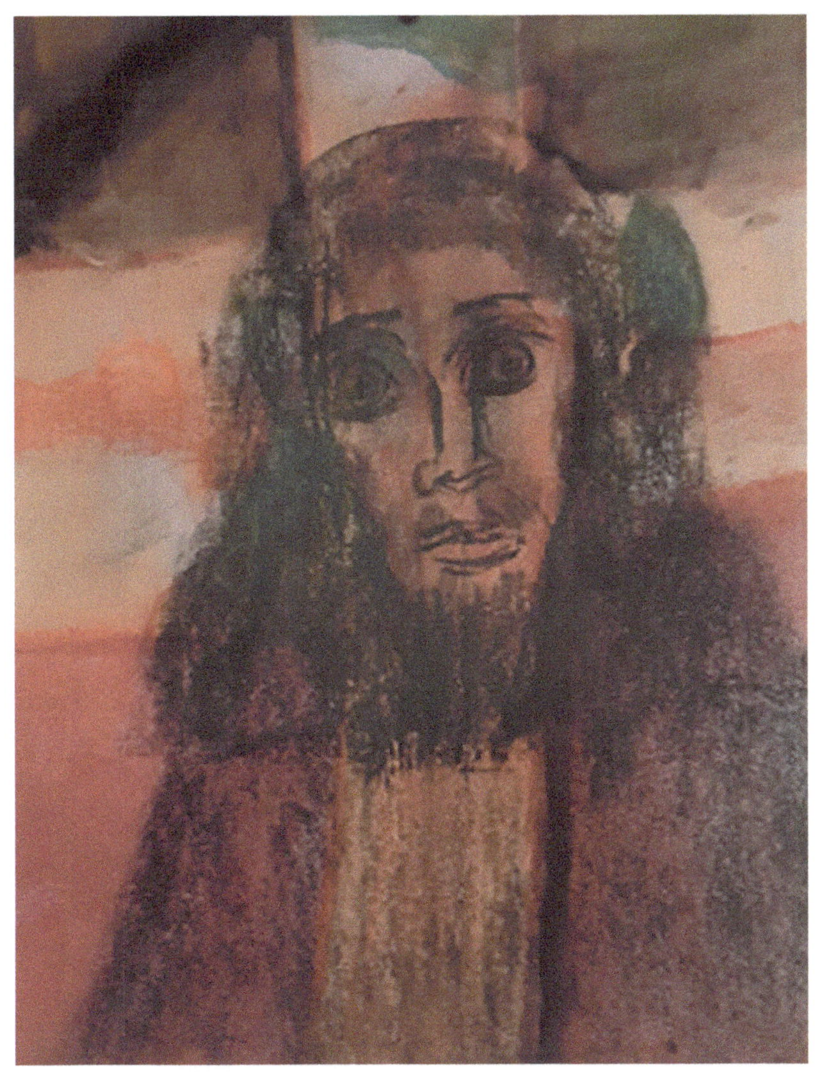

75. *In Love*

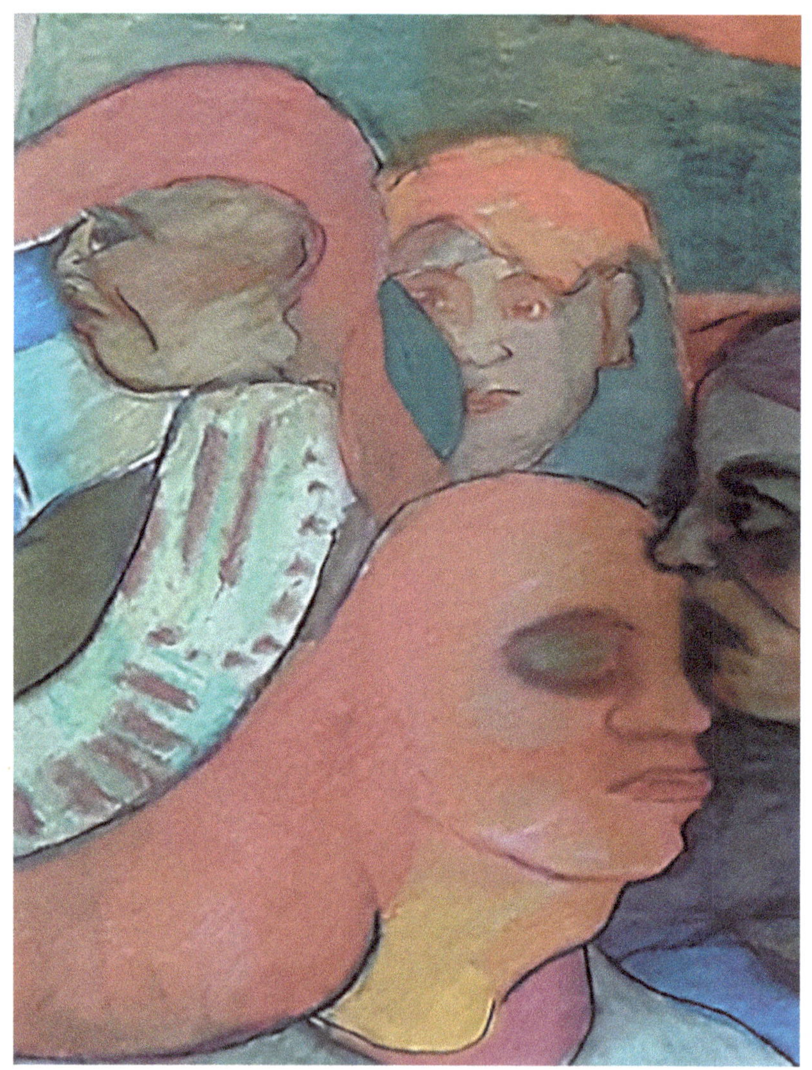

90

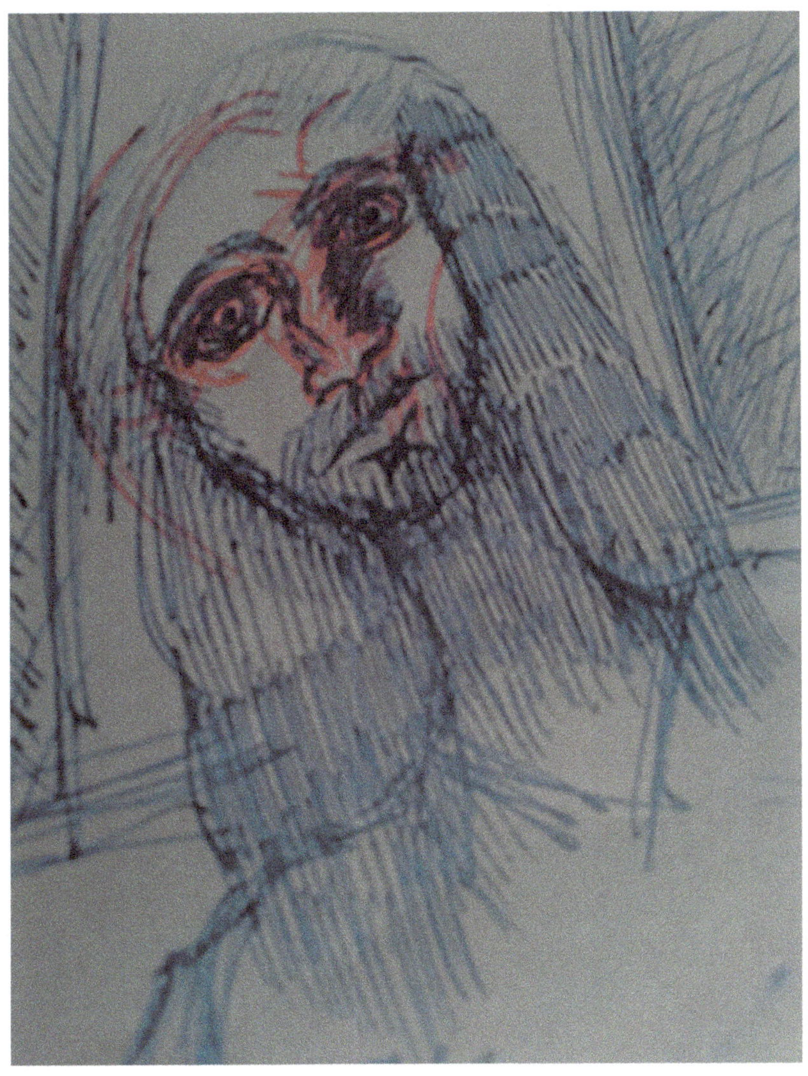

76. Sad Musician

77. Angels

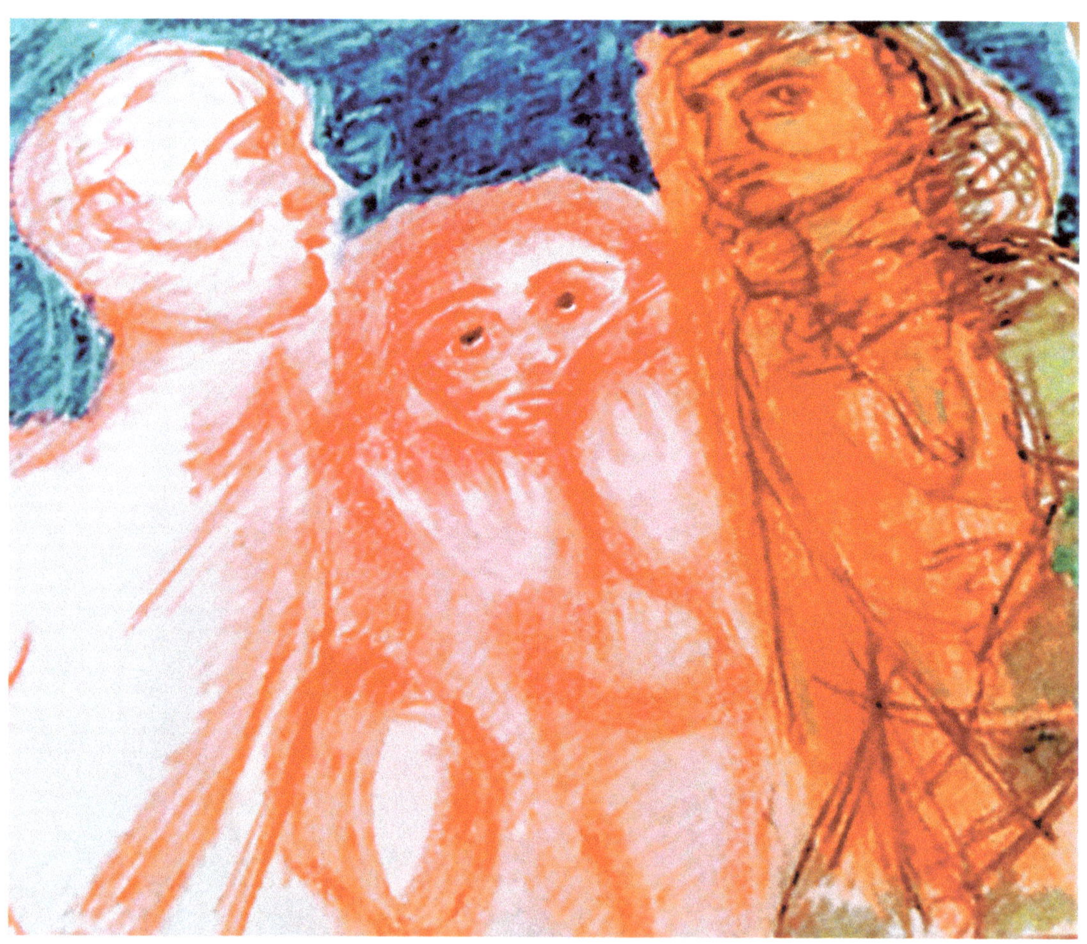

92

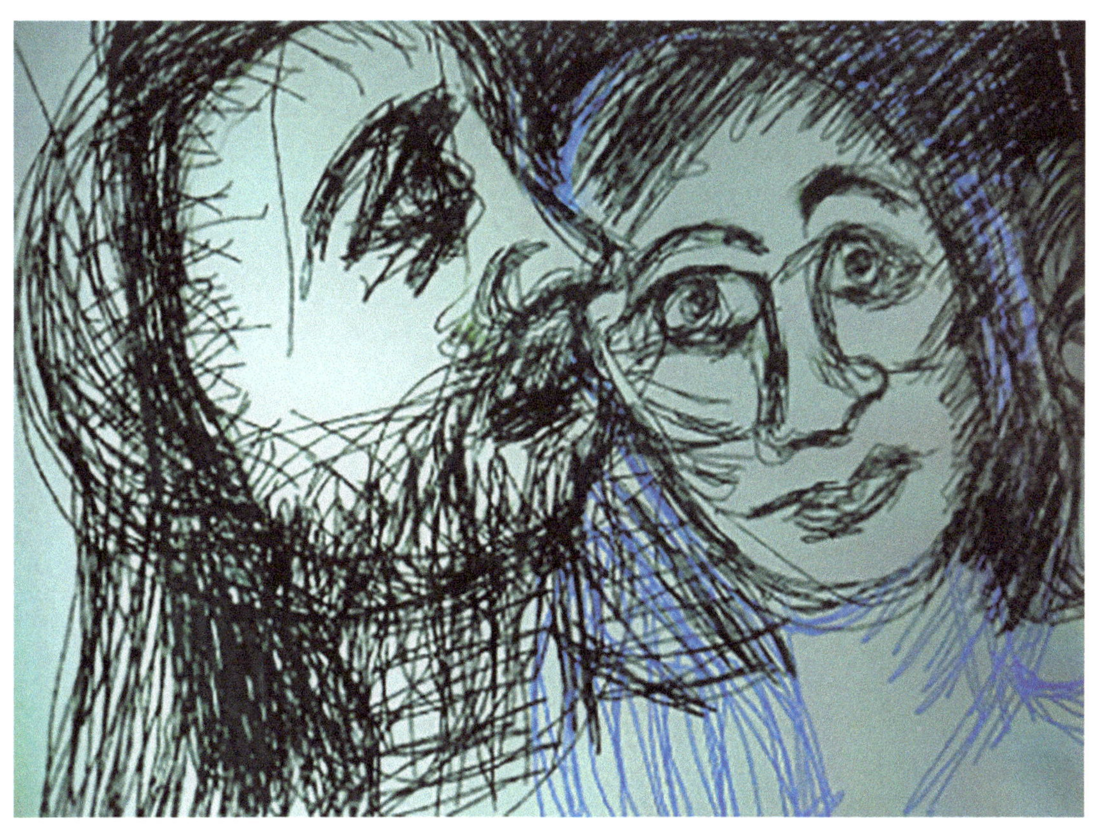

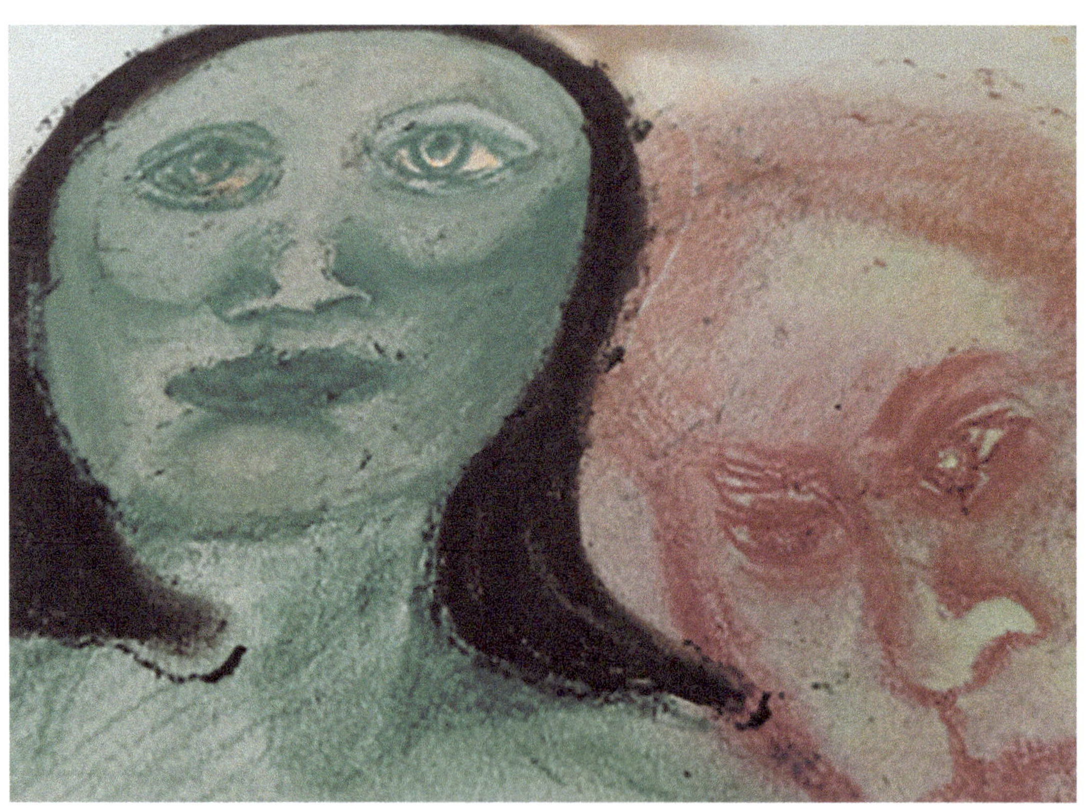

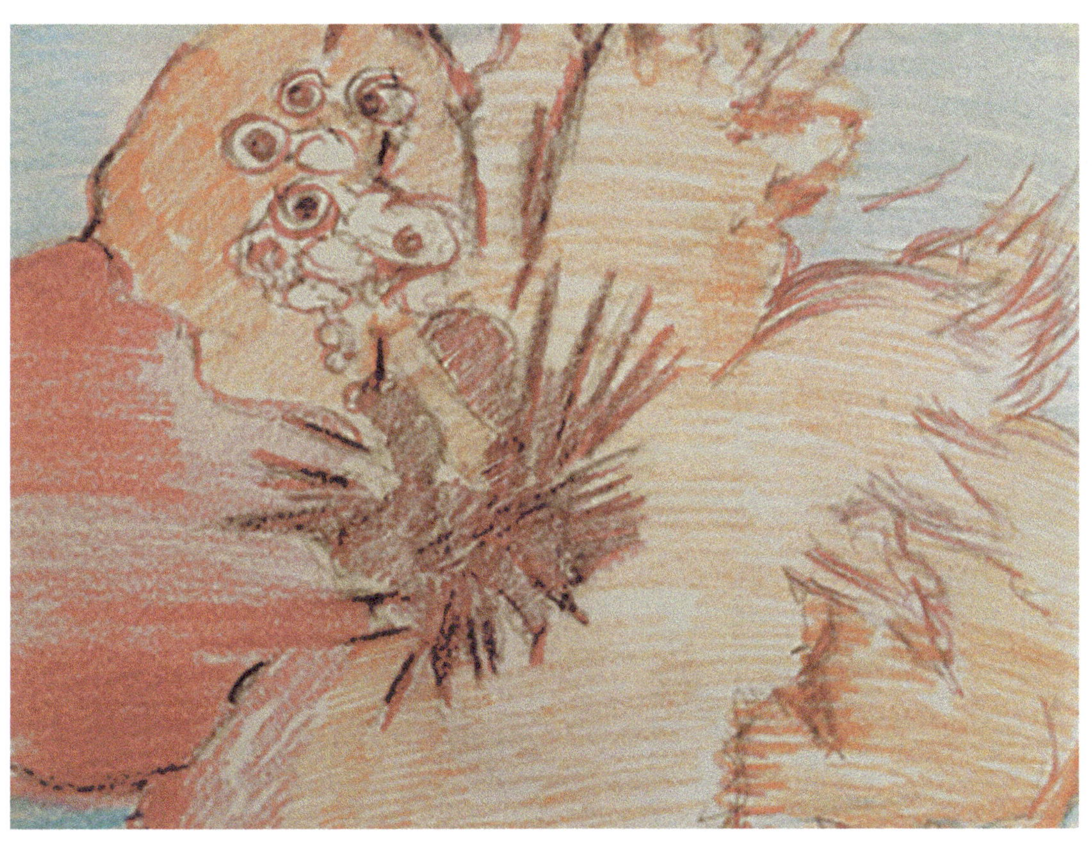

81. *The Spirit of Jesus*

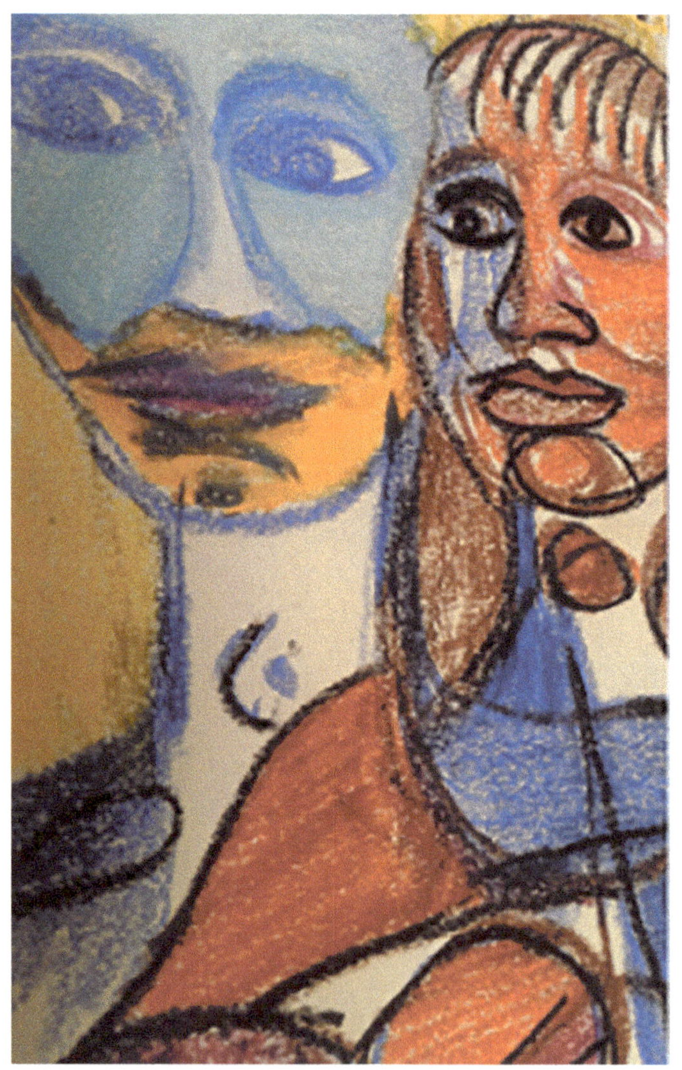

82. Woman Writing

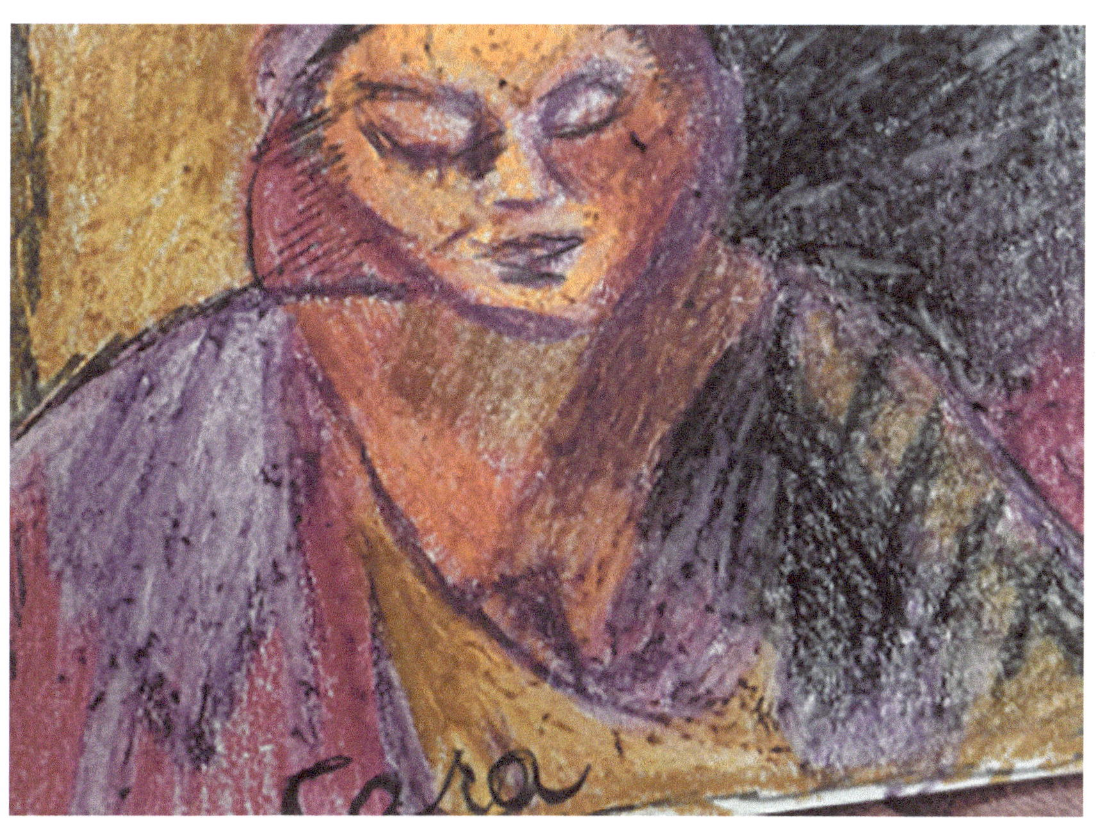

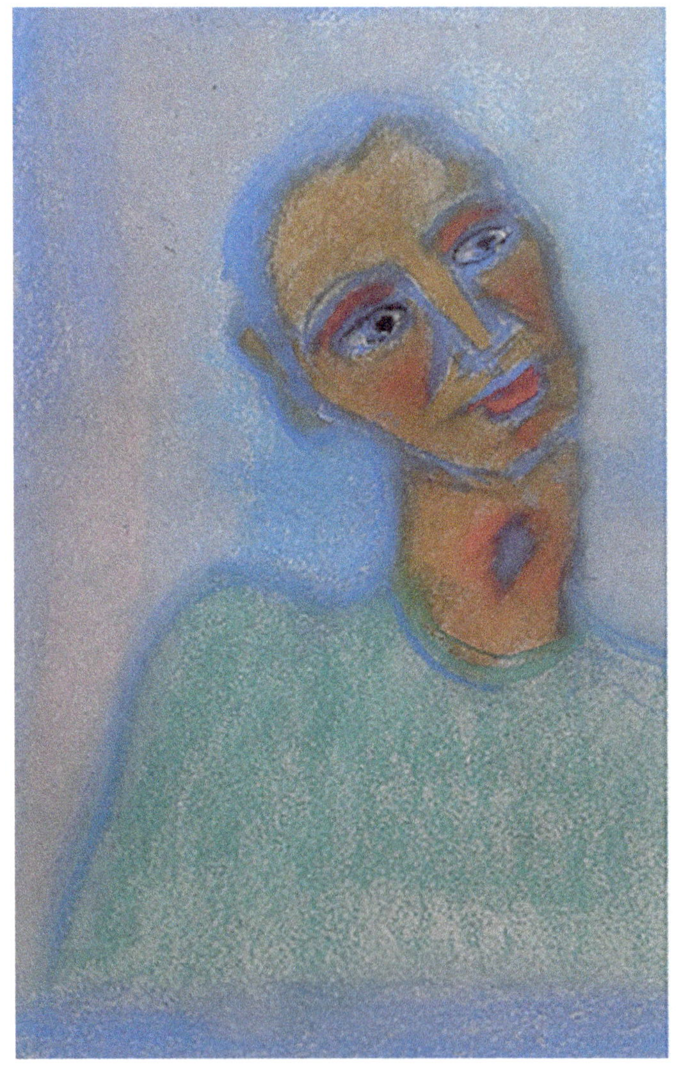

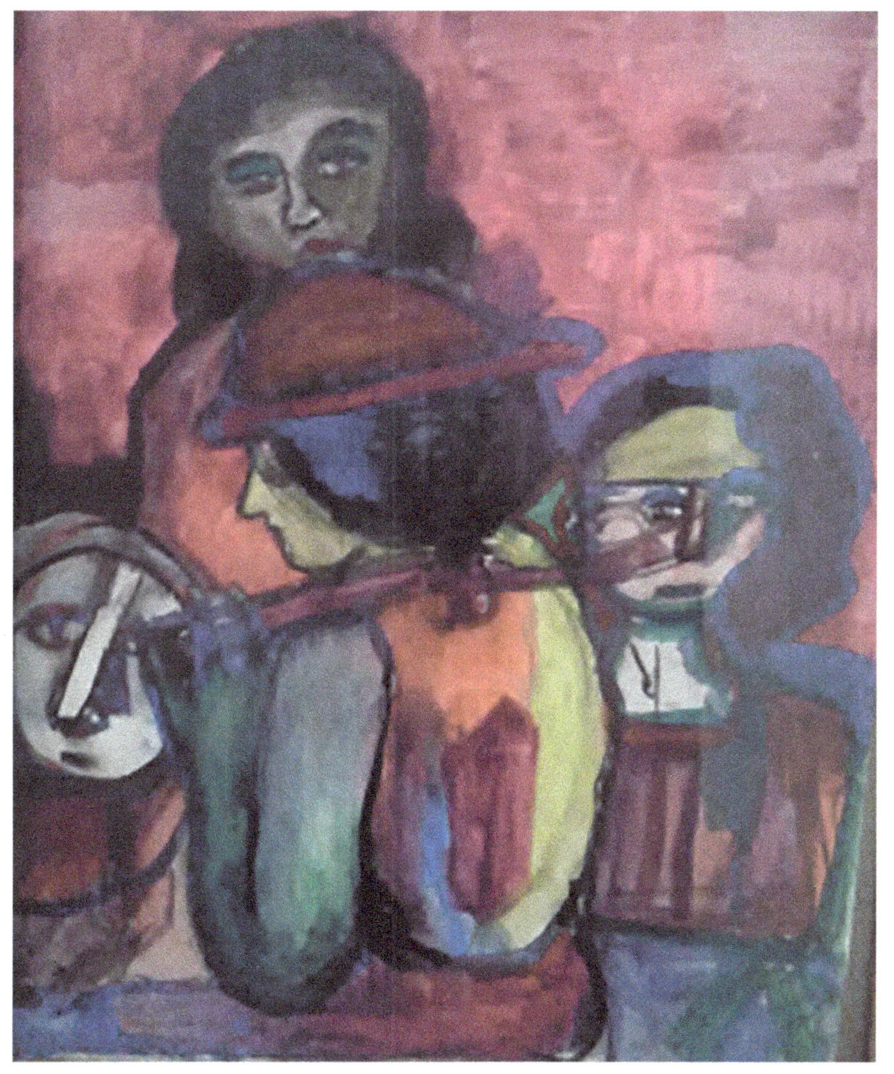

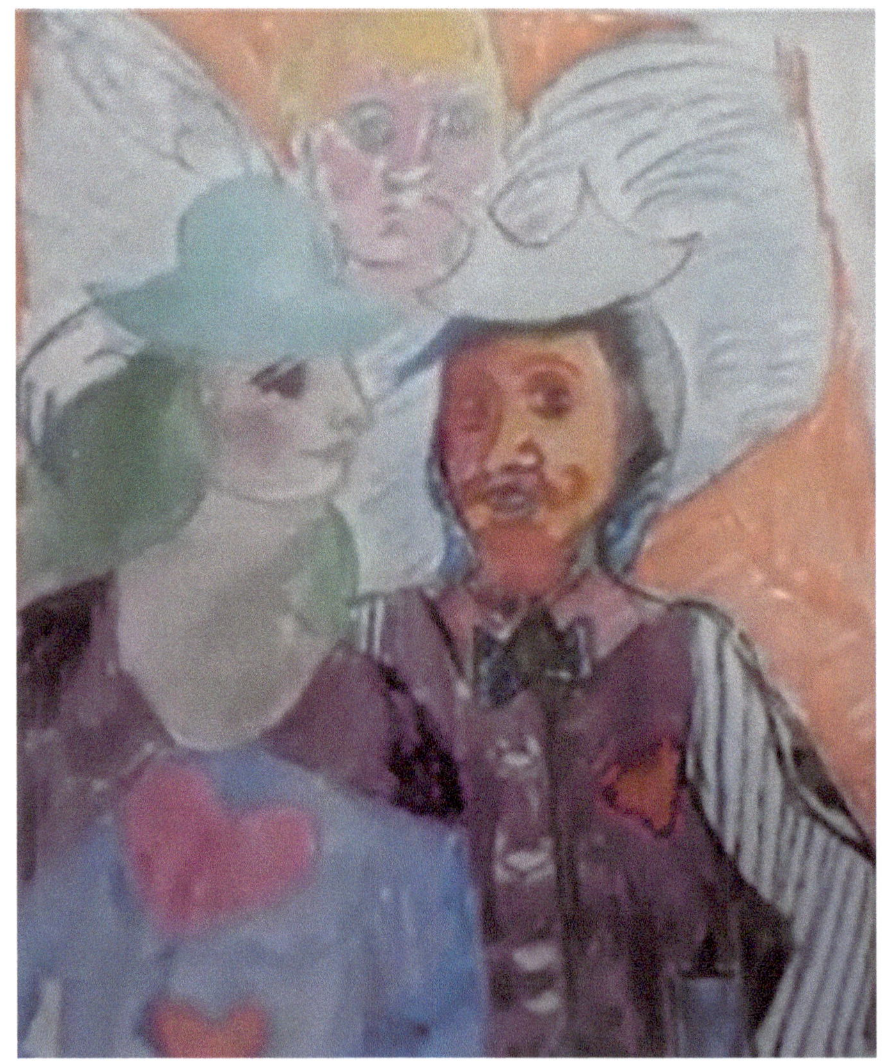

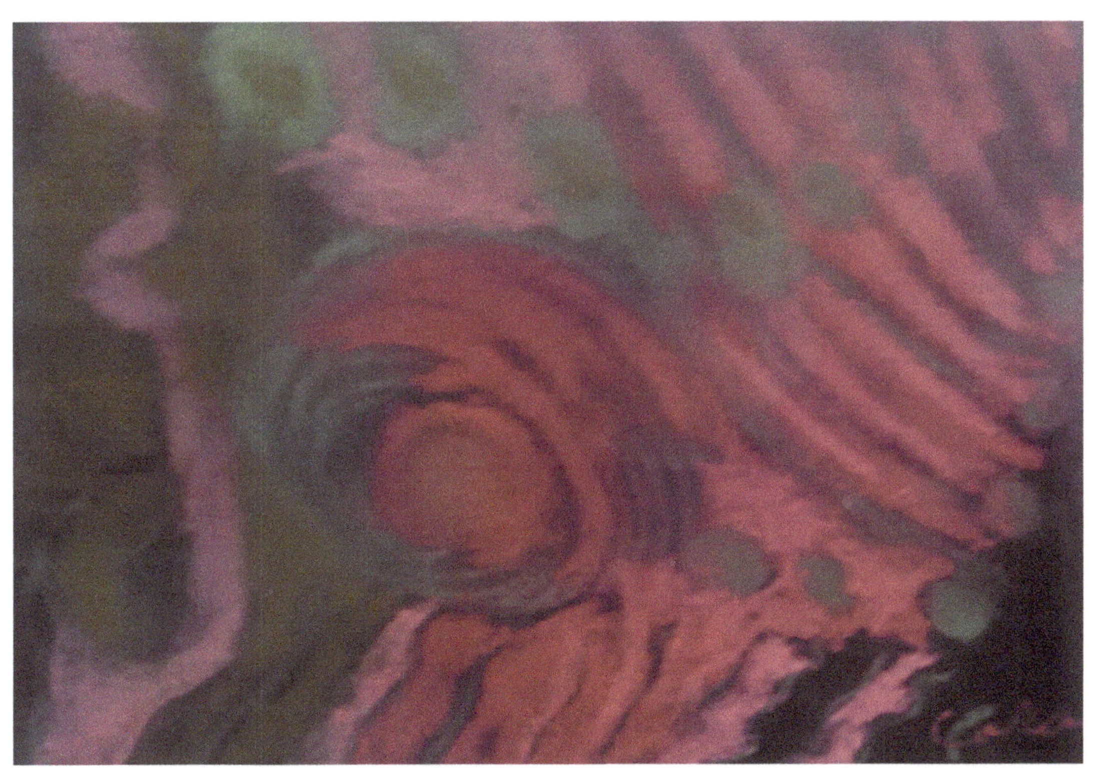

86. Summer Bloom

87. Classic Rose

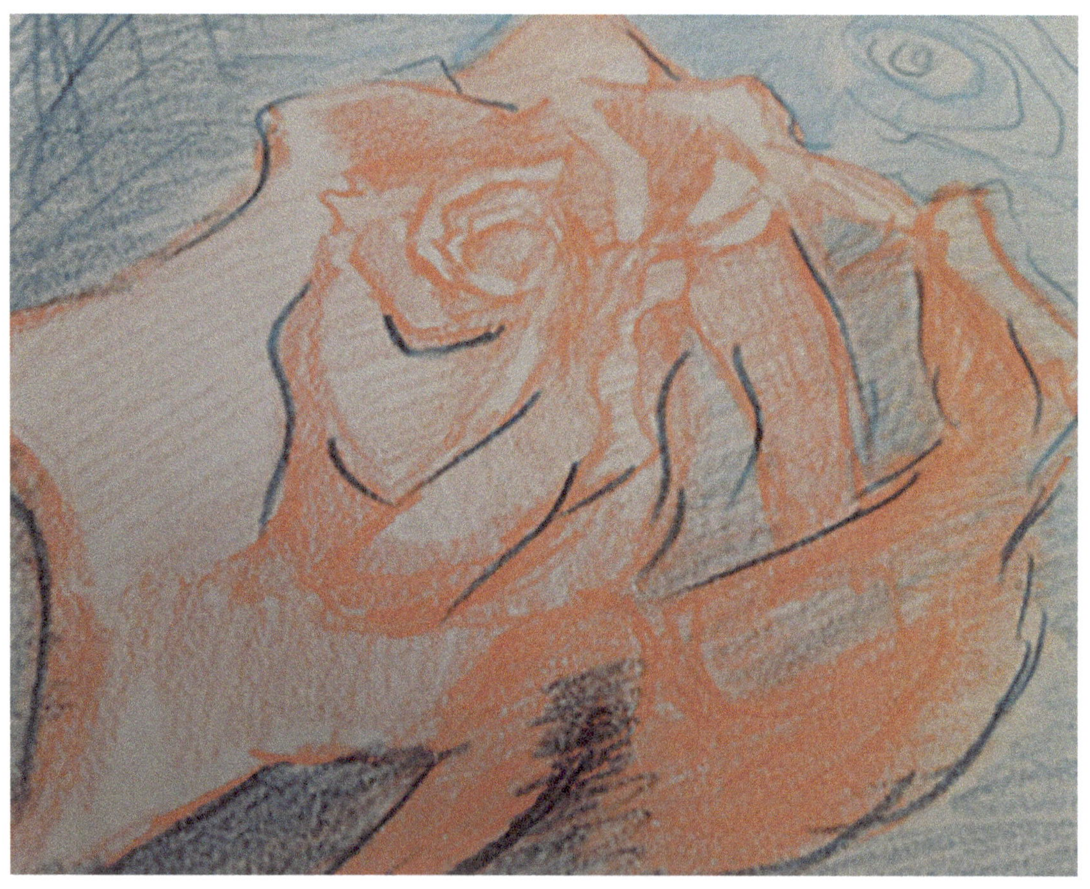

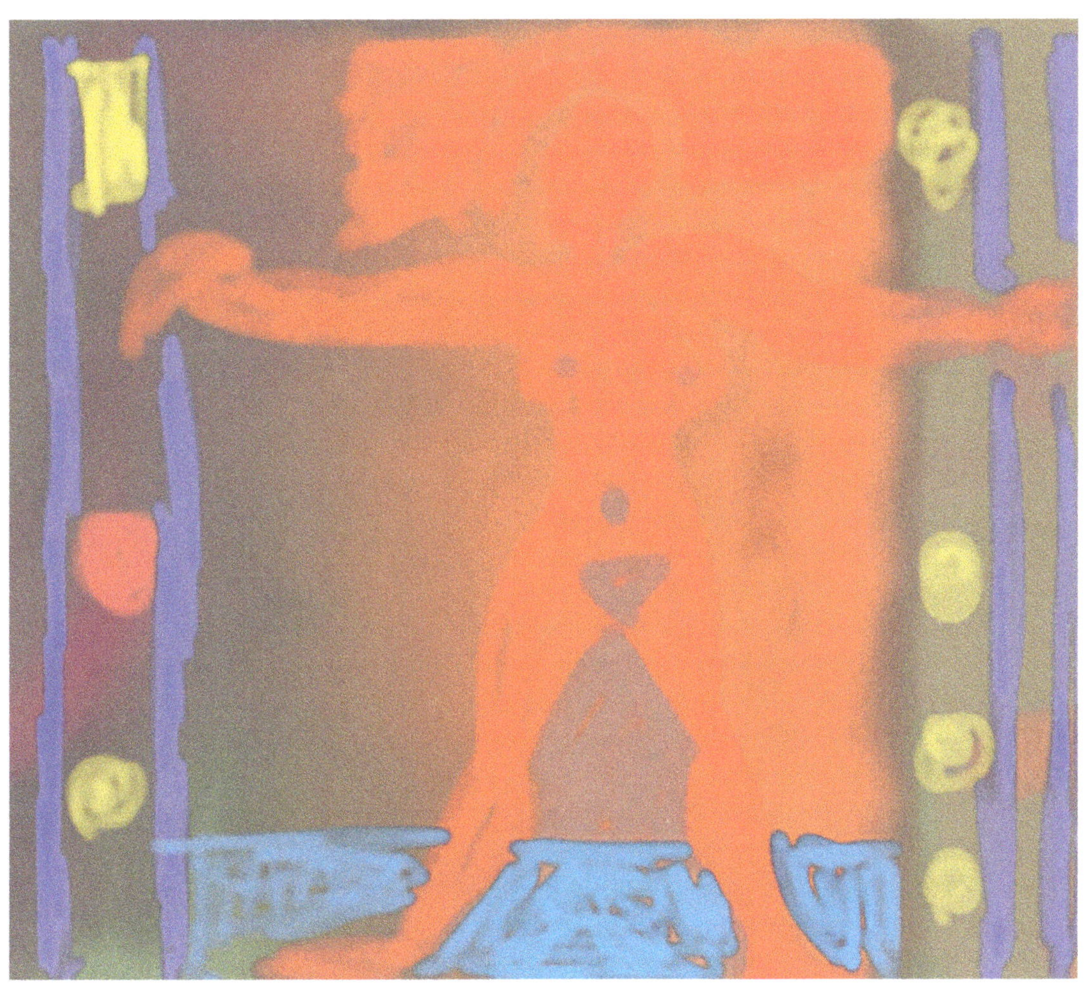

89. *Drawing of Joe*

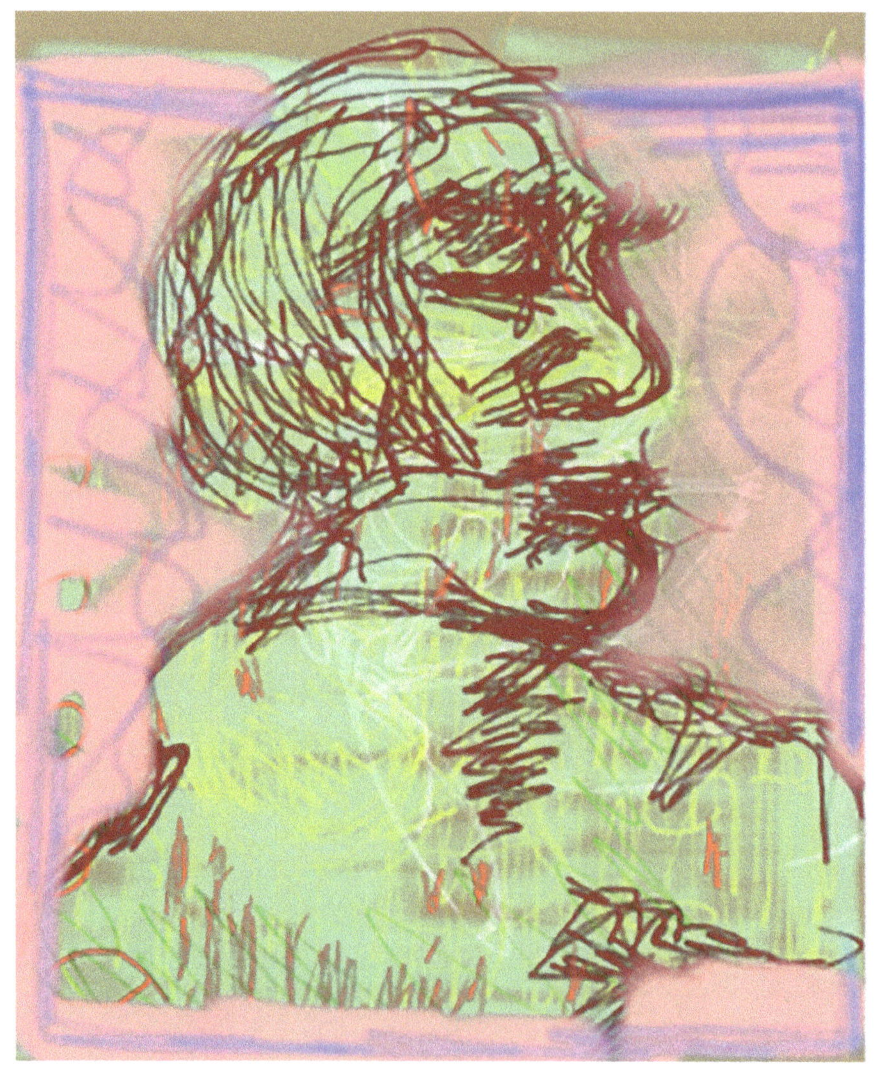

104

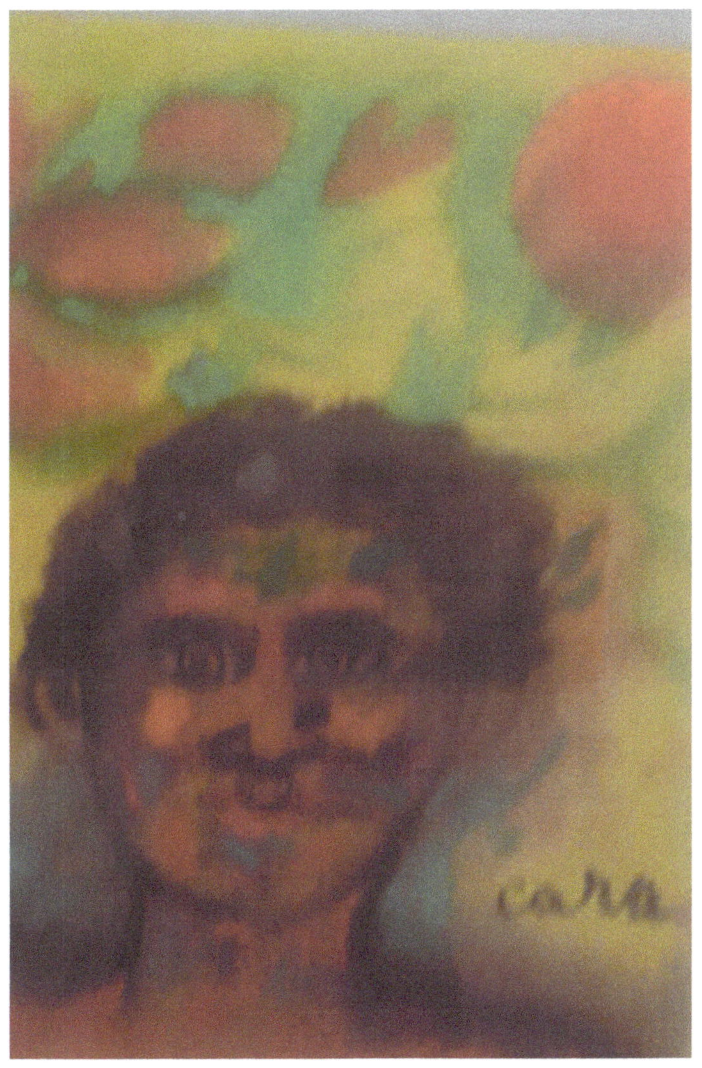

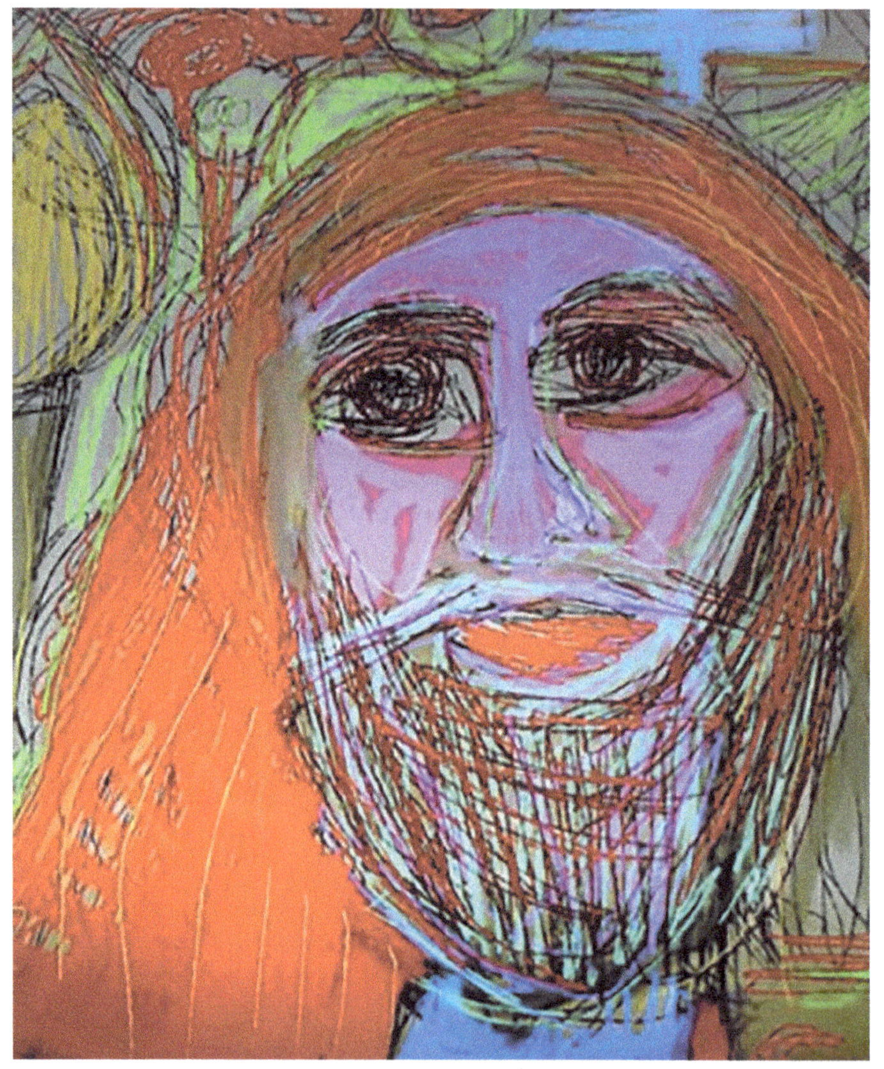

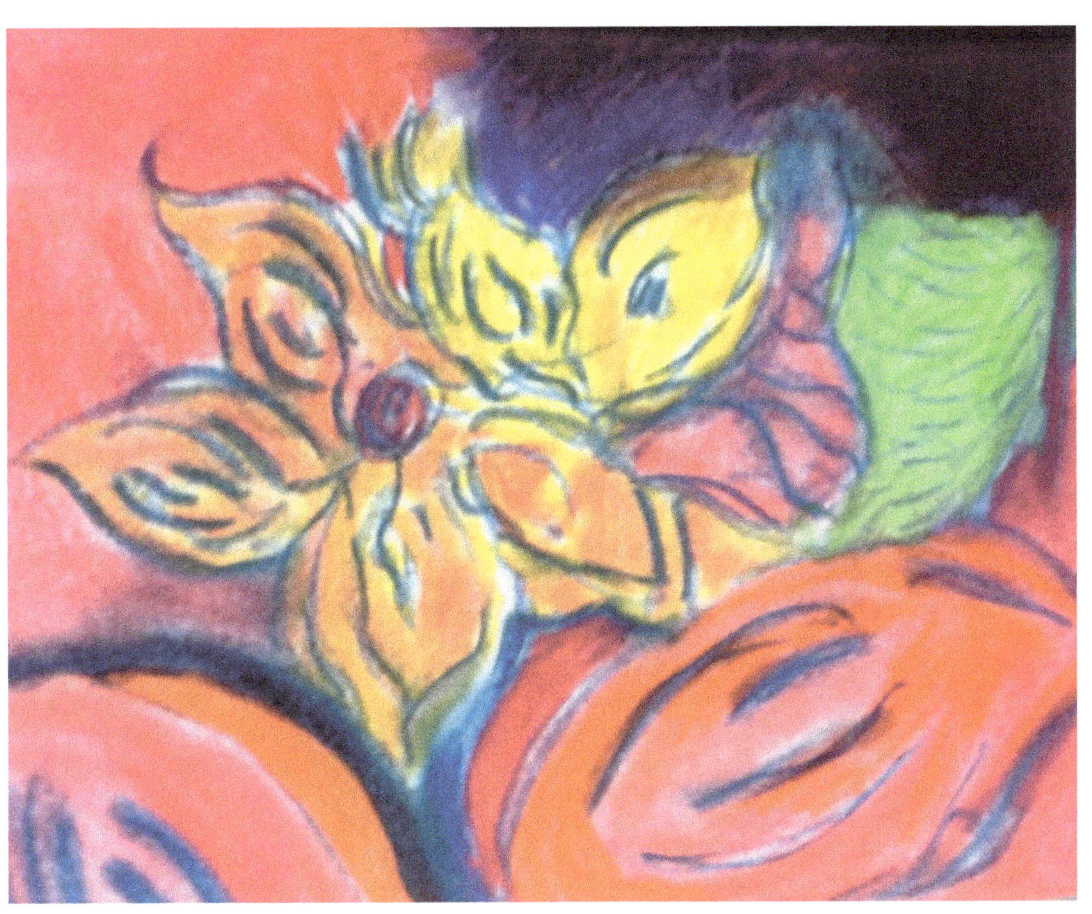

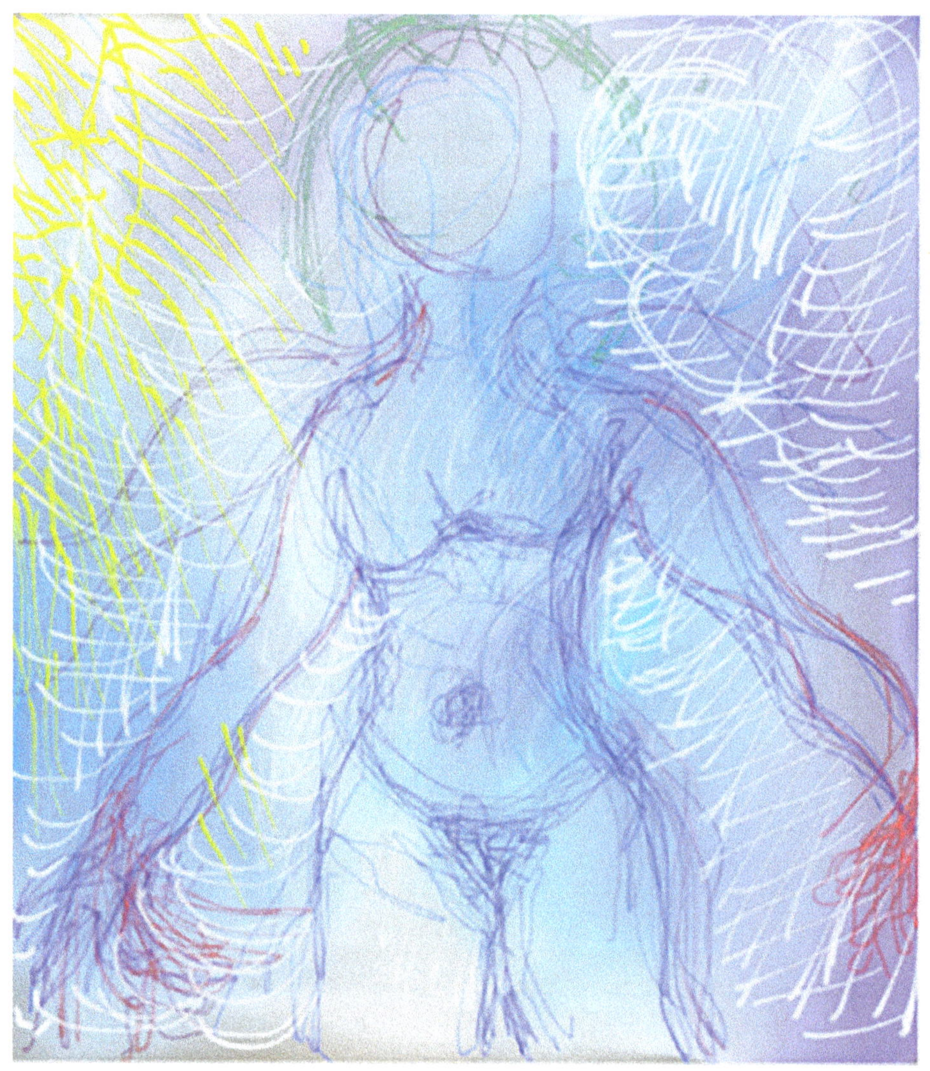

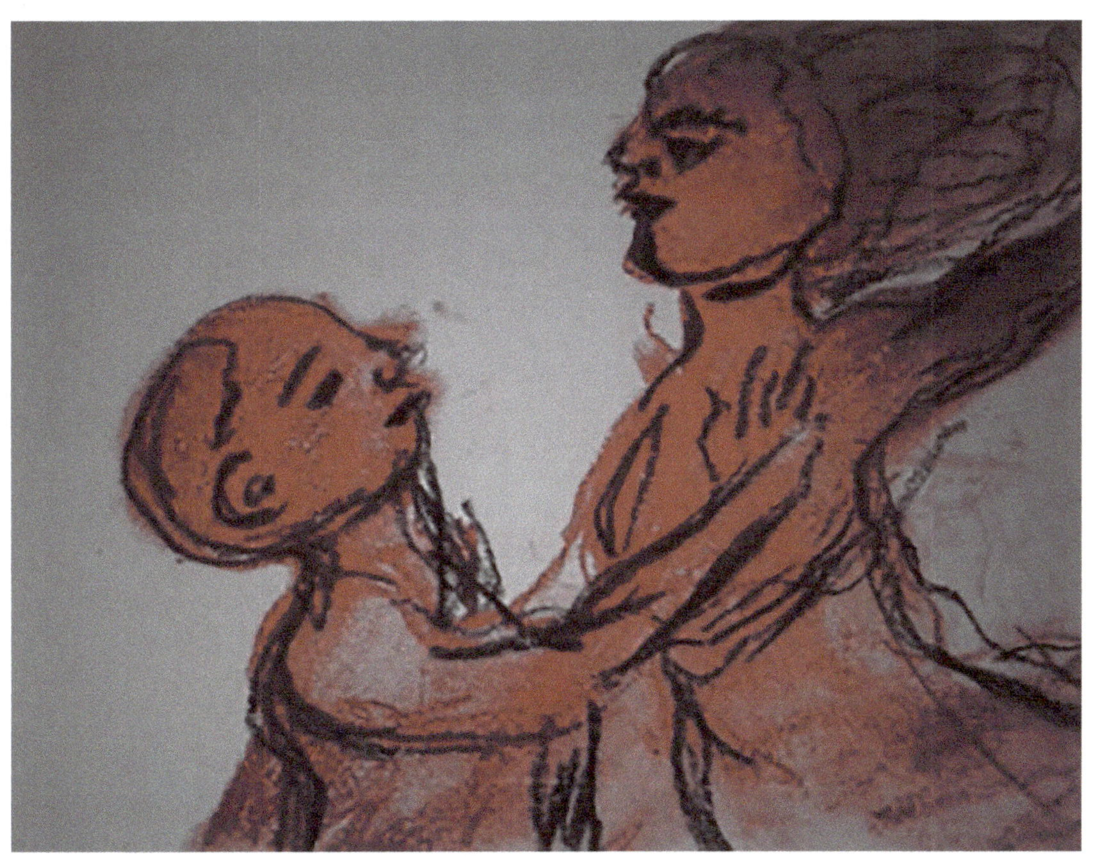

94. Mother and Child, Jubilant

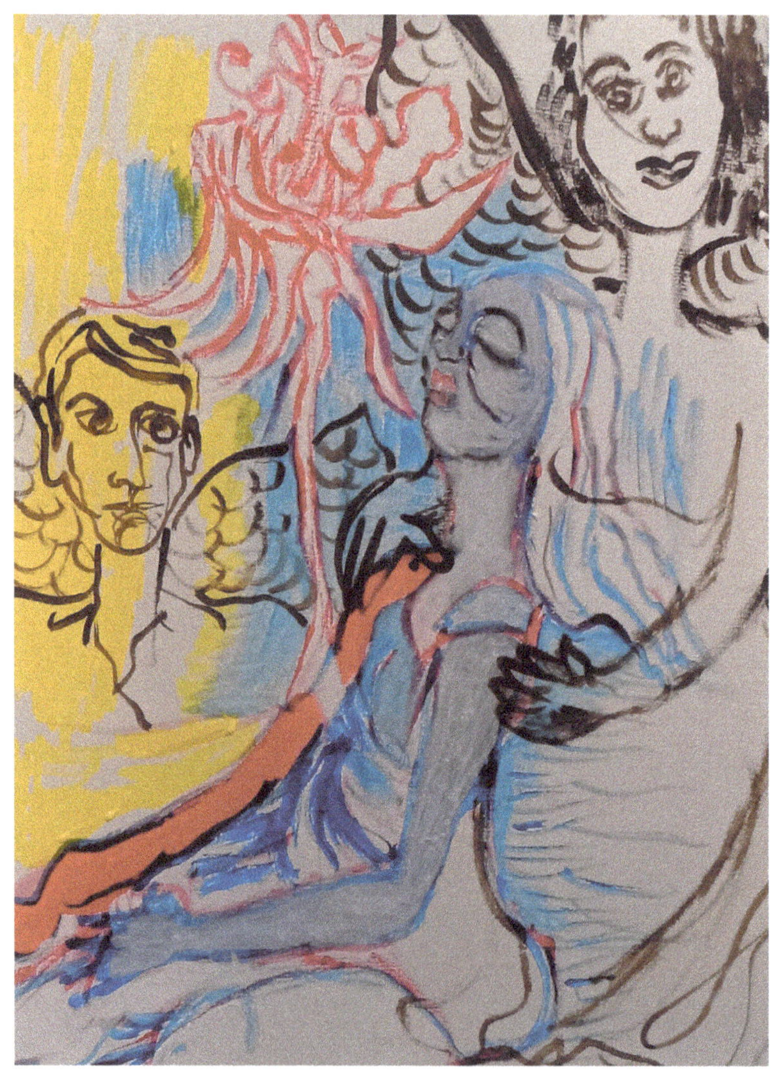

96. Loving

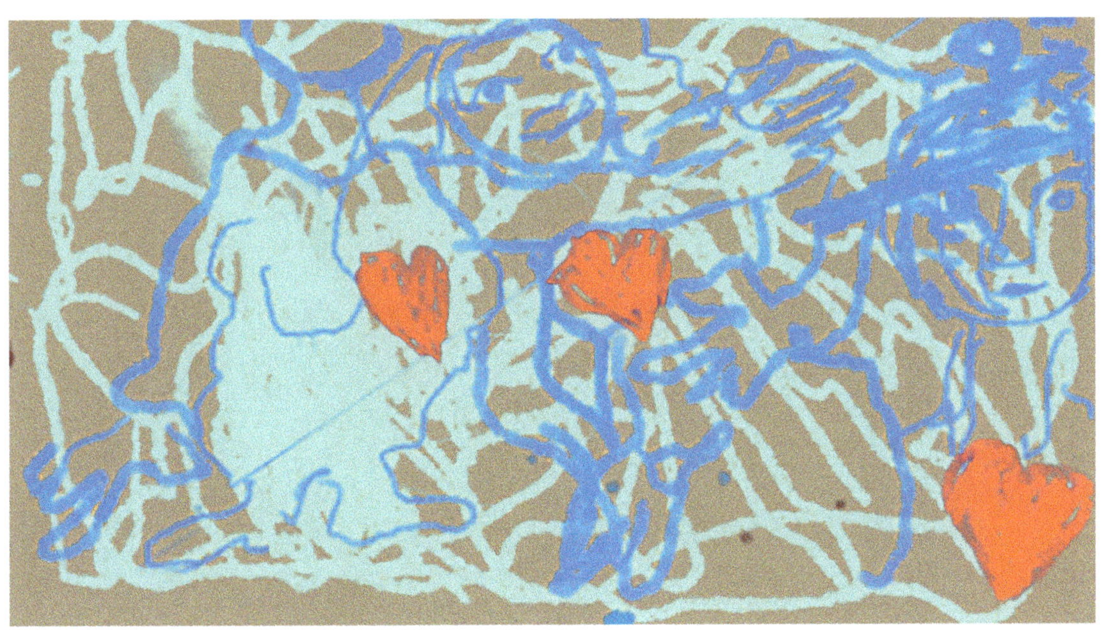

111

97. Gandhi-Like

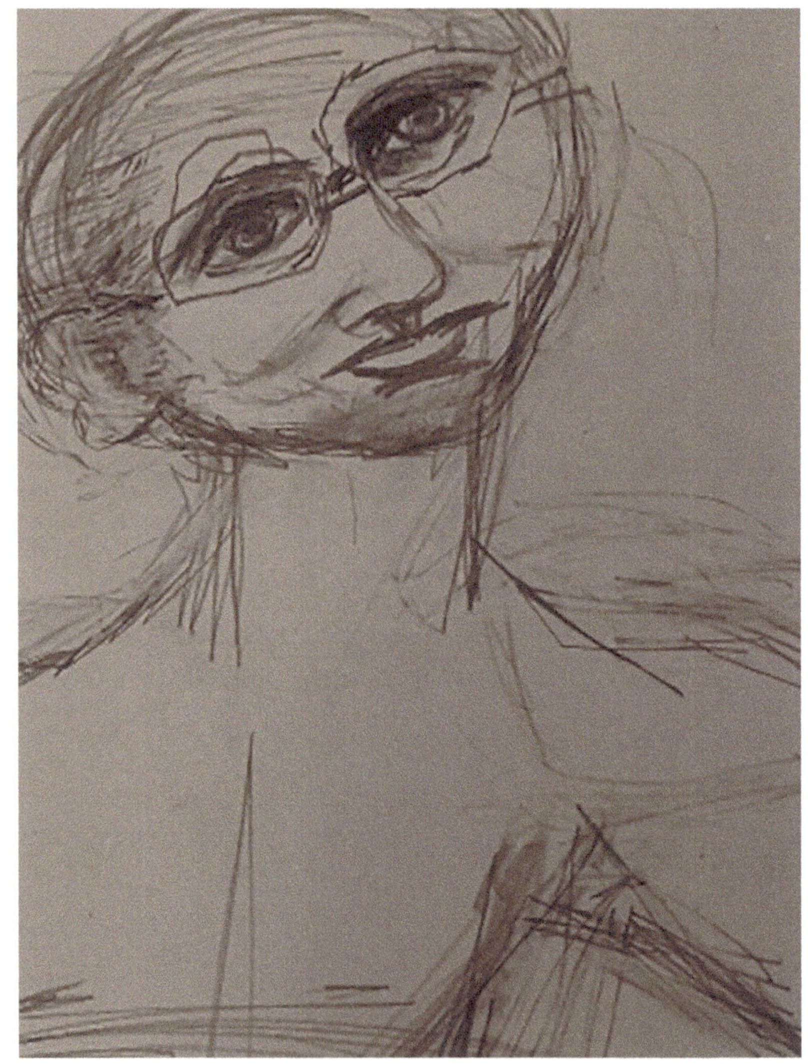

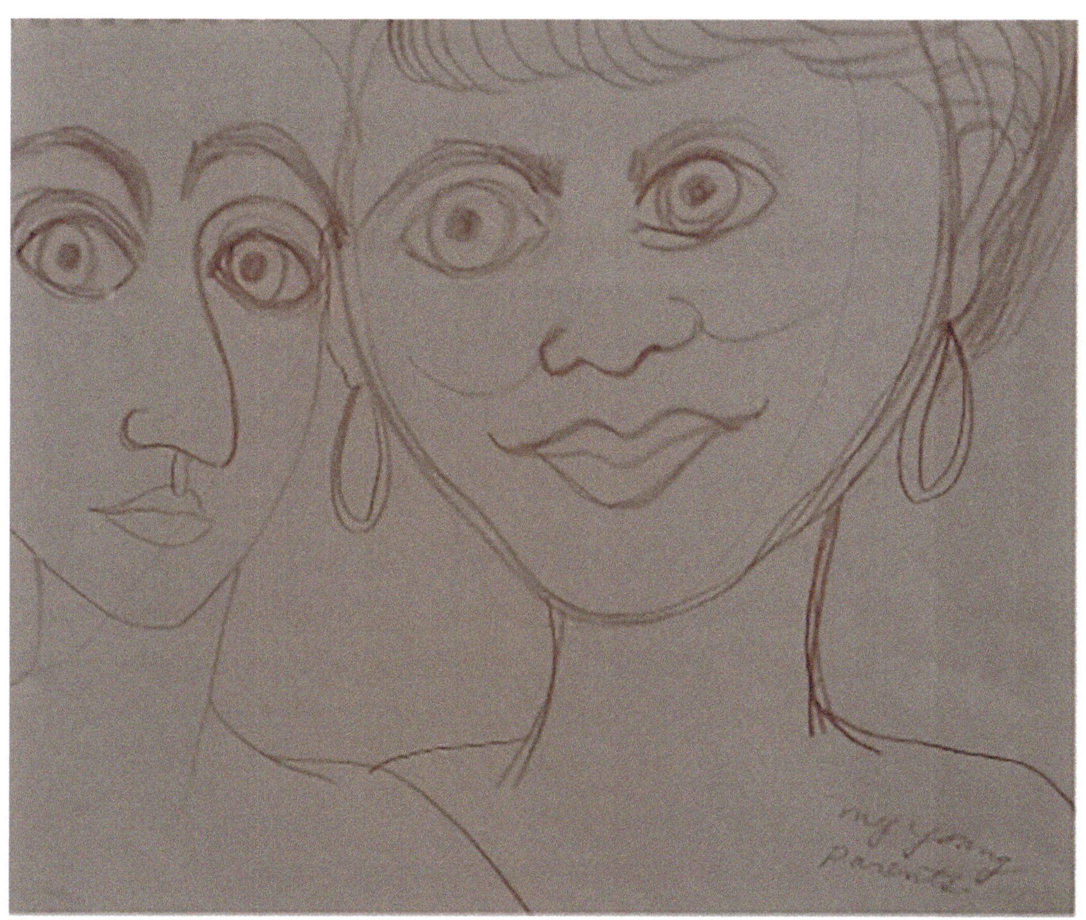

Thank you for giving your sight, mind, and heart to the art of
Dancer Glory.

TO ORDER ADDITIONAL COPIES OF DANCER GLORY

You can purchase copies of this book directly from the website
at the following address:
https://www.rosepress.com/dancer-glory-art-by-cara-berton

TO ORDER PRINTS OF INDIVIDUAL ART PIECES

Any of the images in this book can be purchased as an individual *Giclee* print
using museum-quality media and archival pigment inks. For details, see:
https://www.rosepress.com/dancer-glory-art-by-cara-berton